Chester
Nov.

D1095414

1st   50

Reprinted at 75

WILLIAM FAULKNER
Art in
Theological Tension

WILLIAM FAULKNER

Art in

Theological Tension

JOHN W. HUNT

SYRACUSE UNIVERSITY PRESS

Copyright © 1965
by Syracuse University Press
Syracuse, New York

ALL RIGHTS RESERVED
FIRST EDITION 1965

LIBRARY OF CONGRESS
CATALOG CARD 65-15851

Excerpts from the following Faulkner works have been reprinted
by permission of Random House, Inc.:

Absalom, Absalom!, by William Faulkner. Copyright 1936 and
renewed 1964 by Estelle Faulkner and Jill Faulkner Summers.

Collected Stories of William Faulkner, Copyright 1950 by Random
House, Inc.

A Fable, Copyright 1950, 1954 by William Faulkner.

Go Down, Moses, Copyright 1941 by William Faulkner.

Light in August, Copyright 1932 and renewed 1959 by William
Faulkner.

The Mansion, © Copyright 1955, 1959 by William Faulkner.

Sanctuary, Copyright 1931 and renewed 1958 by William Faulkner.

Sartoris, Copyright 1929 and renewed 1956 by William Faulkner.

The Sound and the Fury, Copyright 1929 and renewed 1956 by
William Faulkner.

The Town, © Copyright 1957 by William Faulkner.

The Unvanquished, Copyright 1938 by William Faulkner.

Manufactured in the United States of America

Composition and presswork by The Heffernan Press of Worcester, Mass.
Binding by Vail-Ballou Press, Inc. of Binghamton, New York.

To my wife Marjorie

Preface

THE dominant literary criticism of our time tries quite legitimately to protect the aesthetic autonomy of works of literature. Because of this, it has placed emphasis upon the close reading of a text and has been reluctant to credit any attempt to use a work of literature as an occasion to discuss "something else." It has identified literature's autonomy as residing in its artistic structure or form, but also, as its great discovery, has seen that form and content, technique and subject matter, are interchangeable terms. Within the last decade and a half, American literary criticism has matured enough to find that to consider what is actually in a work is to consider facts which, from one point of view, have an innate theological dimension, and thus to consider them is not to consider "something else." The sophistication of contemporary criticism consists of more than the argument that a writer's belief imposes structure upon his subject, or that, conversely, his structure determines the subject matter of his belief. Rather, it resides in the recognition that in pursuing the business of his workshop an author unavoidably embodies his private theological vision in the literary properties of the work itself. This vision can be abstracted only by rigorous literary analysis.

Thus it is that the heart of this book is a critical study of three major Faulkner stories. The analyses proceed on the unargued assumption that theological events and meanings are native to the subject matter of literature and are

embodied in its form; specifically, that Faulkner's novels imply the theological matrix from which they spring, and that their form is in part a product of his theological vision. No claim is made that Faulkner is a theologian. He is a literary craftsman of genius whose art, when properly assessed as art, can tell theology something about its own present tasks. This is a book about Faulkner, not a book on theology, and it offers no solutions to the problems analysis of his fiction raises. In short, my aim is not to grind the apologetic axe, but to clarify the theological direction taken by the major American novelist of our time.

I am aware that this study is of a special kind, that it is limited in aim and scope, and that it touches upon only one facet of Faulkner's attraction for us. It is my hope, however, that it will show the theological content of some of our greatest literature is not to be relegated to trivial, prosaic, and therefore easily dismissed literary facts—such as biblical parallels or analogies, or explicitly religious concepts, terms, or events. Because I have tried to stay within the limits close literary appraisal allows, some will be disappointed that I have not quickly enrolled Faulkner on the side of the angels; because I have employed the traditional language of theology and drawn thoughts from contemporary theologians, others may feel I have been too quick to put Faulkner down as one of the saints. My hope is that these chapters will show Faulkner to be a literary master who employs strategies implying a complex theological vision.

In writing even so modest a book as this, one incurs many debts. There is first of all gratitude for what Faulkner has done for contemporary American letters, but, more personally, I am grateful for the many years of discovery and delight which began with my first reading of him while a college student. Not until graduate school was I made aware of how much of my interest in Faulkner had been in the theological decisions implicit in his fiction, and for this lesson I cannot thank Professor Preston T. Roberts of the University of Chicago enough. It was he who taught me that my devotion to literature and deep interest in the problems of theology did not mean I had to live privately or professionally a life of divided loyalties. It was he who first warned me that a too easy identification of Faulkner with the Christian tradition overlooked other theological elements which were there as well. At every crucial point in my study of Faulkner, Mr. Roberts has pushed and guided and corrected me in countless hours of conversation.

When the time came for my ideas on Faulkner to be put down in book form, I was helped by two other friends in ways which only those who know them can fully appreciate. Professor Wayne C. Booth, now of the University of Chicago, was for many years my colleague in the English Department at Earlham College. Perhaps because he is always full of his own work, Mr. Booth unconsciously turns every encounter into a stimulating and trenchant exploration of ideas. His own devotion to literature—his vast knowledge about it and humble joy in it—is apparent to all in his published work. But though he is always enlightening, for me a twelve-hour drive with Mr. Booth from Earlham to the East coast stands as the most sustained and fruitful period I have ever experienced of deeply involved argument and discussion about modern literature. The subject for the day was an early draft of the manuscript for this book, which Mr. Booth had read the day before.

Professor Cleanth Brooks of Yale University is another critic and friend to whom I am in debt. First of all, mine is the debt of any critic who has an interest also in theology, for Mr. Brooks has demonstrated time and again how valuable such an interest can be in opening up a literary text, just as he has also shown the limits within which such an interest must operate. In his characteristically gracious man-

ner, he has also helped in specific ways. His criticism of an
early version of this book encouraged me both to go ahead
with revision and to cut forests of dead wood which hap-
pily will never burden any reader. His love for Faulkner's
fiction and his ability to read a text closely have been too
widely recognized to need any comment.

I wish to thank Random House, Inc., for permission to
quote from the Faulkner books under its copyright, and
Chatto & Windus Ltd. for permission to quote from *A Fable,
Go Down, Moses, The Mansion, The Town,* and *The Unvanquished;* and I acknowledge with thanks the publishers
who have granted permission to quote from the following:
Mysticism and Logic, by Bertrand Russell, used by permis-
sion of Barnes & Noble, Inc. and George Allen & Unwin
Ltd.; *Justine,* by Lawrence Durrell, used by permission of
E. P. Dutton & Co., Inc. and Faber & Faber Ltd.; *Faulkner
at Nagano,* ed. Robert A. Jelliffe, used by permission of
Kenkyusha Limited; *A Theological Word Book of the Bible,*
ed. Alan Richardson, used by permission of The Macmillan
Company and Student Christian Movement Press Ltd.; *On
the Limits of Poetry,* by Allen Tate, Copyright, 1948, by
Allen Tate, used by permission of William Morrow & Co.,
Inc.; "Wilderness and Civilization: A Note on William
Faulkner," by Ursula Brumm, used by permission of *Parti-
san Review; The Symposium,* trans. W. Hamilton, used by
permission of Penguin Books Ltd.; *The Irony of American
History,* by Reinhold Niebuhr, used by permission of Charles
Scribner's Sons and James Nisbet & Co., Ltd.; and *Collected
Essays,* by Allen Tate, used by permission of Alan Swallow.

Thanks are also due to Earlham College and its President,
Landrum R. Bolling, who has created an atmosphere where
scholarship is a free response to dedicated inquiry rather
than a result of professional pressure. I want also to thank
my typist, Mrs. Cora Lee Huntsman, who responded cheer-
fully and expertly to stern requirements that she be perfect.

Finally, I have learned why acknowledgment to one's wife so often appears at the end of a Preface: the debt is so deep that the task of expressing it is put to the last. Fortunately for me, she has not decided to print her thoughts about Faulkner separately. Rather, through years of patience, loyalty, and creative thought she has made herself somewhere present in every major idea of this book.

JOHN W. HUNT

London
November, 1964

Contents

Abbreviations and Editions Used in the Text

AA   *Absalom, Absalom!* (New York: The Modern Library, 1951)

CS   *Collected Stories of William Faulkner* (New York: Random House, 1950)

     A Fable (New York: Random House, 1954)

FN   *Faulkner at Nagano* (Ed. Robert A. Jelliffe; Tokyo: Kenkyusha, Ltd., 1956)

FU   *Faulkner in the University* (Ed. Frederick L. Gwynn and Joseph L. Blotner; Charlottesville, Va.: The University of Virginia Press, 1959)

GDM   *Go Down, Moses and Other Stories* (New York: Random House, 1942)

LA   *Light in August* (New York: Harrison Smith and Robert Haas, 1932)

M   *The Mansion* (New York: Random House, 1959)

     Sanctuary (New York: The Modern Library, 1932)

     Sartoris (New York: Harcourt, Brace, and Co., 1929)

SF   *The Sound and the Fury* (New York: The Modern Library, 1946)

T   *The Town* (New York: Random House, 1957)

U   *The Unvanquished* (New York: Random House, 1938)

WILLIAM FAULKNER

Art in
Theological Tension

The Theological Complexity of Faulkner's Fiction

I

IT IS no longer necessary to make a case for William Faulkner's dominating position in contemporary American letters. Critics have not left his accomplishment to speak for itself but to it have added their own voices. It is more than recognition of his patent genius that has caused them to analyze his literary method, to identify the cultural sources of his art, and to define and redefine his vision. In spite of the warnings of staid professionals to recalcitrant students that no one "does" Faulkner any more, that he has already been "done," students of literature as well as the general reader continue not only to read him and want to read him, but also to feel compelled to make him their own, to "do" him for themselves. For Faulkner communicates a seriousness and a delight which each feels only he can understand and fully appreciate.

Part of Faulkner's continuing appeal has been the private vision projected by his fiction, and it is first of all to an investigation of the theological character of that vision, as one source of the power of his fiction, that this study is directed. My hope is to contribute to an understanding of the degree of theological integrity in his work as a whole. Because what Faulkner has to say to his age is said most effectively in his own mode, the translation, the reduction (criticism is inevitably a reduction) of his art to theological terms will leave a good deal unsaid. But Faulkner himself, in numerous interviews and in such public appearances as his Stockholm Nobel Prize speech, has not been reluctant to speak of his work in what may be broadly thought of as theological terms, and in this way has tacitly invited readers to attend to the theological implications of his art.

The strongest invitation, however, is in the fiction itself. This was recognized in the earliest sound Faulkner criticism when the term "moral vision" was widely used to refer to the constant moral assessment which is an intimate process of his fictive strategy. In those early estimates was an acknowledgment that his world of fiction is bound by a moral thread. In "Faulkner's Mythology" (1939), George Marion O'Donnell, for example, saw Faulkner as a traditional moralist, trying from the tradition to judge modern values. Later, in his "Introduction to *The Portable Faulkner*" (1946), Malcolm Cowley clarified the ethical contradiction referred to by O'Donnell as lying at the heart of the aristocratic tradition, and described Faulkner's positive activity as an attempt to give expression to current moral confusion. Robert Penn Warren's "William Faulkner" (1946) pointed to issues common to the tradition and our modern world which are identified and evaluated by Faulkner in an attempt to define what it means to be human. In 1949 Russell Roth traced in Faulkner a shift from an ethical to a religious concern, from an attention to problems of conduct to an interest in formulating an understanding of the nature of man.[1] Thus Faulkner's Nobel Prize speech of 1950 affected Faulkner criticism more in degree than in kind, and since that time there has been a wealth of critical material taking

[1] The articles by O'Donnell, Cowley, and Warren are most conveniently found grouped together in *William Faulkner: Three Decades of Criticism*, ed. Frederick J. Hoffman and Olga W. Vickery (East Lansing: Michigan State University Press, 1960), pp. 82-124. Roth's article appeared as "William Faulkner: The Pattern of Pilgrimage" in *Perspective*, II (Summer 1949), 246-54.

its cue from the temper of his own commentary on the fundamental character of his work.

But the term "moral" as it has been used encompasses neither all of theology's concerns nor all of the theological concerns of Faulkner. The work of such men as Roth, Walton Litz, Hyatt Waggoner, Cleanth Brooks, Preston Roberts, Nathan A. Scott, Jr., Randall Stewart, John Killinger and others has made it increasingly apparent that Faulkner's religious achievement exceeds even the connotative meanings of the word "moral." In differentiating morality and religion I do not intend an antithesis severing their bond. Between them lies the same distinction obtaining between a doctrine of man and a doctrine of salvation, between anthropology and soteriology. Morality is what man does responsibly for himself to save himself, that is, to make life more meaningful. Or, as Henry N. Wieman puts it, it is conduct aiming at an "order of interrelatedness among people" which will "produce more abundant value in human life than can be produced without it."[2]

Morality approaches religion as it seeks to create the conditions for salvation. Religion involves what God does for man that man cannot do for himself. It is at least moral but it is more than morality. Morality takes on a religious character, and ceases, therefore, to be merely moral, when the kind of meaning or fulfillment or salvation for which it aims receives its definition from beyond itself—put simply, from God's point of view rather than man's. We will discover Faulkner's moral concerns moving toward the religious, for example, when he shows that the moral virtues of the traditional southern society can be fulfilled only if they are transcended, that a spirit essentially different from the traditional is necessary for the attainment of the traditional virtues themselves.

[2] *The Source of Human Good* (Chicago: The University of Chicago Press, 1946), p. 223.

Faulkner's theological center in general and his doctrine of man in particular are at issue here: his perception of God's relation to the nature of things, his insight into the objective and subjective structures of meaning, his feeling for the extent and character of the value inherent in the empirical features of man's experience in the modern world, and his answer to the ancient question of who man is. His theological vision is wide and complex, as broad and varied as the Yoknapatawpha saga itself. In the saga it is not always even, nor is it always profound. Certainly it is not always the same, since he does not always render the same sensibility. Yet there is an essential integrity throughout, for although he may not deal with the same subject always in the same way, the fundamentally theological concerns which drive him to state and restate, to modify, amend, adjust, and reassess the nature of the reality which he presents operate fairly consistently.

II

Faulkner's theologically rich perceptions of reality come to us in the concrete, dramatic mode of a tale being told. Because the way the story is told makes all the difference, it is important to understand the relationship between his storytelling method and his vision. Essentially his method is heuristic, since it forces the reader to stand deeply within whatever individual sensibility is being rendered and to assume with the author some of the responsibility for shaping the materials of the story into a coherent world. In order to produce this effect, Faulkner employs a whole range of rhetorical devices for which he has become famous.

Perhaps most intimately connected with his theological vision is his manner of handling symbol, for it is here that his cognitive interests find their best expression. There is,

of course, the usual use of symbol by which an idea is made
sensually and imaginatively perceptible through its presentation as a recurrent image. Hundreds of these could be
mentioned: in *The Sound and the Fury,* for example,
Quentin's prostration at crucial moments, as in the hog wallow with Caddy, at the time he shot at Herbert Head, when
he met Dalton Ames on the bridge, after his fight with
Bland, and the like; the suspension of movement in the
opening and closing chapters of *Light in August,* in the
closing chapters of *Absalom, Absalom!,* in Isaac's reflections
and perceptions in several of the stories in *Go Down, Moses,*
and in "The Long Summer" section of *The Hamlet;* the
corridors of Christmas' life; Miss Rosa's listening behind
closed doors; Vardaman's fish in *As I Lay Dying,* or Flem's
tie and hat in the Snopes trilogy. The symbolic power of
many of Faulkner's images is increased by their reoccurrence
throughout the body of his work—the image of the search,
for example, and the image of the ledger or of book-
keeping.

There is another use of symbol, however, which is more
distinctive. Almost as if he were illustrating a principle of
process metaphysics, Faulkner ties the meaning of an event
to the manner in which it occurs in the consciousness of a
character. Because the reader is often limited to a character's sensibility, for him, too, ambiguity of fact is con-
joined with a lack of sure interpretation as to significance
of fact. The consequence is an implicit statement about the
constitution of reality itself. One can say of *Absalom,
Absalom!,* for example, that the entire meaning of the backstage action (Sutpen's history) *is how it occurs* in each character's telling of it.

Another outstanding example is found in the second section of *The Sound and the Fury* where Quentin engages in
a fist fight with Gerald Bland. The first knowledge the
reader has of the fight comes after the fact, when Quentin

asks his friend Shreve what happened. The symbolic meaning of the fight is involved with Quentin's reverie about
his sister Caddy and her paramour, Dalton Ames, a reverie
which the reader later realizes not only occurred during the
fight but actually started the fight, causing Quentin to strike
Bland. The specific function of the scene is to show a certain
quality of Quentin's sensibility, but the impressionistic technique by which it is presented, that is, the presentation of
the effect prior to its cause, also suggests a certain understanding of the reality involved: what is real for Quentin
is the past as interpreted in the present, while the present
itself can become real only when later interpreted. The fight,
which occurs in the chronological present, becomes real, and
therefore can take on meaning, only after the fact. This incident calls attention to the unity of Faulkner's method with
the vision of reality he is rendering at that point in the novel.

Faulkner's revelation through character of the symbolic
dimension of events allows not only for an impressionistic
rendering of the experiencing subject and, by the reader's
involvement, the identification of reader and character in
the experiencing of the event, but also for an expressionistic
rendering of the abstract meanings of the symbolically func-
tioning reality. By his control, in other words, Faulkner is
able to probe intensely the subjective side of experience
and at the same time keep the focus of the reader, through
the eyes of character, upon the meaning of the outward
reality.

III

One important clue to Faulkner's theological center,
then, lies in his presentation of different realities through
character. Because the novels of his great productive period
from *The Sound and the Fury* of 1929 to *Go Down, Moses*

of 1942 were the ones to which critics gave their first serious attention when describing his "world," it has become an almost unchallenged assumption that his private vision is to be identified with the vision of the type of character who was thought to dominate his novels during that period. Some of this misunderstanding strikes one as willful, as arising from rather petty motives or from blind hostility to the early Faulkner. The general attitude of readers who reacted this way—and there were many who did not—was that for Faulkner all is only decadence, chaos, and violence.

One need not deny that psychologically driven, haunted, and confused people populate his novels, but it is a mistake to conclude that his characters are confused because he is himself confused—that, as one critic, Sean O'Faolain, has said too recently to be overlooked, "the frustrated characters are projections of his own defeat."[3] Why O'Donnell made a similar judgment is easy to understand. His estimate preceded O'Faolain's by seventeen years and was balanced by a sympathy for Faulkner's larger fictional strategy. Indeed, violence, with its implication of chaos and decadence, stands, in the larger view, as an index to the integrity of Faulkner's theological center. To conclude that these distressing elements are there because Faulkner himself is "at home only in this murky, demonic world," or because "his psyche is completely out of his control," or because he is exploiting sensationalism for money, is to miss the total vision in which these obvious qualities of his world take on the symbolic function of laying bare the moral nerve ends of the present human condition.

I do not mean to beat a dead horse, for in spite of the fact that too much recent Faulkner criticism begins by taking a swipe at the early critics who were hostile or simply missed the point, Faulkner criticism is now, by and large,

[3] *The Vanishing Hero: Studies in Novelists of the Twenties* (London: Eyre & Spottiswoode, 1956), p. 131.

sophisticated enough to be judicious about Faulkner's relationship to his characters. Yet the strange fact remains that
even those who showed early sympathy with his fiction contributed to misunderstanding. One of the finest French
critics, Claude-Edmonde Magny, whose discussion of Faulkner's style will always be a landmark in Faulkner criticism,
describes Faulkner's universe as "the world before the Incarnation, completely absorbed in the contemplation of what
was, occupied in marking time, in tirelessly scanning the
records of its past glories." Magny goes on to ask, "How
could it not appear desperate, when hope is not yet with
it?"[4]

There is some advantage in this view, though in many
ways an eschatological image such as the one Yeats describes
in "The Second Coming" would be more accurate, and one
is grateful for the suggestive way Magny deals with the
evidence which led less perceptive readers to cries of horror.
For if one avoids her mistake of identifying Faulkner's theological vision with that of his lost characters, the description
of his world as post-Fall and presalvation or as in the last
days of a still fallen condition clarifies some fundamental
features of his whole vision. It explains the mythic quality
of his total performance, and accounts for the presence of
violence and decadence as signs of an evil inevitable for a
world which is pre-Incarnation or for one in which the first
Incarnation has failed in its promise and the second Incarnation has not yet come. In such a time all is by definition
on the decline.

But most suggestive in Magny's thesis is the implication
for Faulkner's view of time and for the related problems of

---

[4] "Ainsi l'univers que nous propose Faulkner c'est le monde-d'avant-
l'Incarnation, tout entier absorbé dans la contemplation de ce qui fut, occupé
à marquer le pas, en scandant inlassablement les fastes de ses gloires révolues.
Comment ne paraîtrait-il pas désespéré, puisque l'Espoir n'a pas encore lui?"
"Faulkner ou l'inversion théologique," *L'Age du roman américain* (Paris:
Editions du Seuil, 1948), p. 210, translated by W. H. Bowen.

the locus and availability of meaning. In an unredeemed world or in a world in which man finds himself unable to accept the proffered redemption, time is not the same as in a world with a sure and meaningful future. For Quentin and Hightower there is no hope because there is no true future. Time is "the mausoleum of all hope and desire" (SF, 95), a tomb entrapping the evil and folly of human experience, an abstraction which desensitizes present reality. For Dilsey and Lena Grove, on the other hand, time as such presents no problem. It is not a tomb for the dead weight of the past, but the texture of experience, the context in which the concrete facts of life are met and made meaningful, are endured and found redemptive.

In a reality which is only creation and fall there is nothing upon which to focus the attention except the corrupt and unredeemed creation itself; a search for value and meaning can lead only to the past, to the time between the creation and the fall when the creation was without taint and the hope had not gone out of it because man's pride had not alienated him from nature and himself. In such a reality value and meaning have no other place to reside except in the past. This much explains Quentin's obsession with the tradition and his effort to find some act sinful enough to establish that there is something worthwhile in the present because there is some value that can be outraged. It explains why Hightower is only "a single instant of darkness in which a horse galloped and a gun crashed" (LA, 465) and why he violently rejects Byron Bunch's request that he implicate himself in Christmas' salvation. It also explains Faulkner's general attraction to the past, not as a tomb, but as the possible locus of values which can function as normative for what man can achieve in the present.

Another French critic, Jean-Paul Sartre, is out of sympathy with the implied metaphysics in Faulkner's presentation of time because he, too, identifies Faulkner's vision with that of his lost characters. Where there is no future and no present there is no freedom: Faulkner, says Sartre, has "decapitated" time; he has "taken away its future—that is to say, the dimension of free choice and act."[5] Sartre is, of course, raising these objections from the point of view of the existentialist belief that man *is* only insofar as he acts —"existence is prior to essence." The existentialist's emphasis is upon the present moment as it moves toward the future, for only in the act is moral reality established and freedom gained. It is not surprising, then, that Sartre cannot believe in the Faulknerian man—Faulkner's man is "just a matter of lighting"—and that he charges that Faulkner's world is not true.[6] For those of Faulkner's characters who are unsure of an objective truth of any kind, it must be said that their world is not true; no world is true; no world *can* be true—all one has is a piece of it, a vague notion.

Sartre's objection is that Faulkner's world does not correspond in any way to reality. The events of his illusory reality seem literally, as Sartre says events never do, to "pounce upon us like a thief."[7] Events discover the character rather than vice versa, as Ratliff says in *The Mansion* (134); they are just suddenly there, unexplained and mysterious, and begin to take on a fixity as they begin to be recalled or as their causes are revealed by a recapitulation from several points of view. Without warning, in *Light in August,* for example, we are told:

> The arm which she held jerked free. She did not believe that he had intended to strike her; she believed otherwise, in fact. But the result was the same. As he faded on down the road, the shape, the shadow, she believed that he was running. She could hear his feet for some time after she could no longer see him.

[5] "Time in Faulkner: *The Sound and the Fury,*" trans. Martine Darmon, in *Three Decades,* p. 230.
[6] "William Faulkner's *Sartoris,*" *Yale French Studies,* No. 10, p. 95.
[7] Sartre, in *Three Decades,* p. 232.

> She did not move at once. She stood as he had left her, motion-
> less, downlooking, as though waiting for the blow which she
> had already received. (177)

In this passage we are not told by flat statement that Joe
Christmas struck Bobbie Allen. We begin to know it and
finally are told of it after we have been introduced to her
interior state. The constant amaze of so many of Faulkner's
characters in the face of some event illustrates the same lack
of a real present. Sometimes a character will find himself
completely temporally dissociated from the event in which
he is involved. At one point, Joe Christmas

> seemed to be turned in upon himself, watching himself sweating,
> watching himself smear another worm of paste into his mouth
> which his stomach did not want. (*LA*, 114)

Temple Drake, in *Sanctuary,* experiences a similar detachment:

> For an instant she stood and watched herself run out of her
> body, out of one slipper. She watched her legs twinkle against
> the sand, through the flecks of sunlight, for several yards, then
> whirl and run back and snatch up the slipper and whirl and
> run again. (109)

Obviously, Sartre is right about the relative absence of a
present and a future in Faulkner's reality. His objection
amounts finally to an unwillingness to accept as possible a
fallen world in which the will is obliterated. Since in such
a world all reality is past reality, the literal future is fixed
and the efficacy of the will is denied. Joe Christmas, *before*
he entered the house to murder Joanna Burden, "believed
with calm paradox that he was the volitionless servant of
the fatality in which he believed that he did not believe.
He was saying to himself *I had to do it* already in the past
tense; *I had to do it. She said so herself"* (*LA*, 264). In
this as in many other scenes, what will happen seems already

to have happened. Christmas waits with "astonished fatalism" (114) to be caught in the dietitian's clothes closet. He delivers himself to be arrested in Mottstown, furious that his pursuers do not catch him more quickly. Mink Snopes in *The Mansion* assumes he has already killed Houston: "*Maybe I ought to waited till he* [his cousin Flem] *got back* he thought, turning at last back to the now empty and vacant platform, noticing only then that he had thought, not *should* wait for Flem, but should *have* waited, it already being too late" (35). In *The Sound and the Fury* Quentin assumes his suicide to be a fixed fact and thus his narrative point of view is at the point of death. The children of "That Evening Sun" share with Nancy the conviction that she is as good as dead. When they leave her sitting before the fire waiting for Jesus, her husband, to kill her, Quentin asks, "Who will do our washing now, Father?" (*CS,* 309). Even the redeemable if not redeemed world of Isaac McCaslin in "The Bear" is in tension with a fallen one. Isaac "should have hated and feared Lion. Yet he did not. It seemed to him that there was a fatality in it. It seemed to him that something, he didn't know what, was beginning; had already begun. It was like the last act on a set stage" (*GDM,* 226).

Thus although Magny and Sartre make the mistake of seeing the part as the whole, they do allow us to understand some important aspects of Faulkner's theological vision. And it must be admitted that Magny's view, or the eschatological one I have suggested, has the further merit of introducing an appropriate metaphor, since Faulkner freely employs the Christian tradition to describe the human situation. In fact, in a long argument with Cass in Part IV of "The Bear," Isaac constructs a theological argument in the form of an interpretation of history to explain the signs of evil in his own experience. Man is guilty of the original sin of pride, Isaac believes, manifest as the desire to possess the Negro and the land which was given to all men in common. The

act of pride alienates him from God, and brings self-aliena-
tion as well, and expresses itself in the violence of men's
relationships. Alienation became absolute in America's case
when the last chance was given for a new Eden and the
old corruption in man destroyed it.

IV

One should not infer from the mere presence of
Christian language that Faulkner's theological responses
are Christian. (Magny surely intends no such conclusion—
if anything, in her view Faulkner is more Hebraic than
Christian.) His use of images and terms from the Christian
story does not make him Christian any more than his use
of "Christ symbolism" in such disparate figures as Benjy
and Joe Christmas makes them "Christ figures." *The Sound
and the Fury* does exhibit a Good Friday to Easter Sunday
pattern and is evidence of Faulkner's readiness to use the
structure of the Christian story and even the trappings of
the Christian faith when they present themselves as useful
tools. For anyone interested in his relationship to the particular content of the Christian faith, however, *Light in
August* would appear at first glance to be *the* book of his
early mature period to study, for in it he seems to have
pulled the stops on the use of Christ symbolism.

It is easy to caricature the novel. The Lena Grove–Byron
Bunch line of action opens *Light in August* with a west-
ward journey of the pregnant Lena who trusts "with un-
flagging and tranquil faith" (4) that the Lord will see to
it "a family . . . [will] all be together when a chap comes"
(18), and closes the book with a mother and a child and
a substitute father still on the road in pursuit of the real
father. During the course of the novel, in humble circumstances the eternal virgin and earth mother, Lena, gives

birth to a man-child. Mrs. Hines, witnessing the birth, confuses the newborn infant with her grandson, Joe Christmas,
and thus the point of connection with the second strand of
narration, Christmas', is established. Indeed, it was in his
cabin that the birth occurred, on the very day of his death
and, preposterously, of his resurrection.

Christmas' own parentage and blood are mysterious, his
childhood hidden. His mother by adoption, Mrs. McEachern,
washes his feet; his father by adoption, Simon McEachern,
teaches him by slow, methodical, deliberate beating "that a
stable floor, the stamping place of beasts, is [not] the proper
place for the word of God" (140). As an adolescent he
washes his hands in the blood of a sheep. At the age of
eighteen, "Christmas, the son of Joe" (364) is found by
his parent, not in the temple but in a dance hall; he kills
his foster father (apparently), and runs for fifteen years
into strange lands with no place to lay his head, consorting
after his fashion with publicans and sinners, coming at last,
at the age of thirty-three, back to the South where, after a
three years' stay, he is lynched by those who had been can-
vassing about "for someone to crucify" (272).

Before he murders Joanna Burden, Christmas has an
agony in the garden outside her house. But Joanna's own
story is also told in images and phrases familiar from the
story of Christ. Her "naked breast . . . ached as though in
agony, virgin and crucified"; she prays that the cup might
pass from her: "Dear God, let me be damned a little longer,
a little while" (250); and she visualizes her heritage, her
"burden," in a symbolic image of the white race crucified
for its sins upon a black cross. After he murders her, Joe
wanders aimlessly for a week, feeling lost from the orderli-
ness of time yet experiencing an "urgent need to strike off
the accomplished days toward some purpose, some definite
day or act" (317). At last he sets his face toward Mottstown, not aware that it is the home of his grandparents,

sensing it appropriate when he learns it is Friday that he now enter the town and accomplish the purpose of his days. "It was as though," the townspeople thought afterwards, "he had set out and made his plans to passively commit suicide" (419). When caught, Joe does not resist, even though Doc Hines, his grandfather, shouts to the crowd, "Kill him. Kill him" (327).

Light in August thus lends itself easily to the game of discovering extensive Christian parallelism and is rivaled in this respect only by *A Fable,* which is admittedly structured on the Christian story. With a variation here, an inversion there, a parallel circumstance in one instance and an ironic twist in another, Faulkner makes the trappings of the Christian story leap out at the reader. One critic has even noticed that Joe Christmas is resurrected symbolically after three days in several episodes of his life;[8] another, that "several of Joe's acts take place on Friday, or 'on the third day.' "[9] A third claims "Christmas's Negro and white blood represent the dual nature, human and divine [!], of Christ,"[10] and a fourth has seen Simon McEachern as Simon Peter, Percy Grimm as the Roman soldier who pierced Jesus' side, Lena as Mary, Byron as Joseph (because he works at a planing mill, Byron is somehow a carpenter), Lucas Burch as Judas, and Hightower as Pontius Pilate.[11] One can go even further—many have—in pursuit of Christ symbolism, but suffice it to say that it is obvious, inescapable, and sometimes simply obtrusive.

Light in August embodies Faulkner's theological center

---

[8] Phyllis Hirshleifer, "As Whirlwinds in the South: An Analysis of *Light in August*," *Perspective,* II (Summer 1949), 235.

[9] Richard Chase, "The Stone and the Crucifixion: Faulkner's *Light in August*," *The Kenyon Review,* X (Autumn 1948), 547.

[10] Jerome Gavin, "*Light in August:* The Act of Involvement," *The Harvard Advocate,* CXXXV (November 1951), 37.

[11] Beekman W. Cottrell, "Christian Symbols in *Light in August*," *Modern Fiction Studies,* II (Winter 1956-1957), 207-13.

in ways other than his palpable use of Christ symbolism might lead one to suspect. Yet its use at the hands of critics clearly raises the general question of what such symbolism means for serious theological criticism of the entire Faulkner corpus. Two things are of note. In the first place, Faulkner has made no attempt to conceal the Christ symbolism and has therefore almost invited the violence done to his work by symbol hunters. Certainly he cannot be held responsible for their excesses, but it is understandable that the excesses do occur. A hasty reader is tempted to make Faulkner's writing all dogma, even though it may be heretical, or to interpret his inclusion of Christ symbolism as a typically skeptical attack upon Christianity, or, finally, to resist both temptations and yield to another, either ignoring the Christ symbolism or accusing Faulkner of bad writing.

Unsophisticated Christian readings of Faulkner are reprovable because they get in the way of a full appreciation of his literary achievement, which makes his theological achievement worth study. They also estrange or at least intimidate serious secular critics who do not want to be identified with those who go through Faulkner's novels with New Testament in hand. This last fact is merely regrettable, for the more confident secular critics who have refused to be intimidated, such as Lawrence E. Bowling, Herbert A. Perluck, R. W. B. Lewis, Cleanth Brooks, Robert Penn Warren, or Ilse Dusoir Lind, have shown that theological readings can be made to the advantage of the general reader and certainly to the advantage of Christian apologists who come to Faulkner precisely because he is engaged in a theologically exciting dramatization of the human condition. That much of the best formal criticism discusses Faulkner with reference to the basic themes and issues of which theology speaks, does not mean that the secular critic has sold out to the theologian; it means he has found that to talk about Faulkner he must talk about Faulkner.

It is interesting in this connection to note that in the second part of his introduction to *William Faulkner: Three Decades of Criticism* (1960), Frederick J. Hoffman finds "it can quite clearly be maintained not only that in the last decade critics have explored what Faulkner 'has been driving at,' but that they (or many of them) have been investigating his 'moral vision' and the manner and degree of his resemblance to and departure from Christian thought." "The tenor of recent criticism," Hoffman goes on to say, "is concerned to measure Faulkner's fiction against his public statements, or to explore his analysis of contemporary moral practice, or to make remarkable inferences from the coincidences in it with the Christ story" (31).

Hoffman himself seems to fall among those whom I have characterized as the intimidated secular critics. In his introduction he is, of course, discharging a reportorial function, but at points and moments he does not hesitate, between the lines, to point the finger at critics such as Hyatt Waggoner, Walton Litz, and Nathan A. Scott, Jr., who have simply read what is there in Faulkner to be seen by all who have eyes to see it. Hoffman does, however, finally offer absolution to critics who have not yet strayed to the secular fold, because, as he puts it, "it is a pardonable mistake to make, an error really of emphasis, since Faulkner had all but challenged his critics to make it. For while he had stressed so heavily the moral intention of his work, he had also placed its implications of doctrine within reach of a Christian interpretation" (33).

The usual method of avoiding coming to terms with Faulkner's theological interests is to claim him as a humanist in such a way as to imply that humanism is a position unto itself, devoid of theological ties or presuppositions. Perhaps it is here that the greatest theological naïveté of much criticism lies. It is instructive to discover that so careful a critic as Hoffman himself, to whom all Faulkner criti-

cism is in debt, provides one of the more startling examples
of a failure to discern the religious presuppositions of
humanism. In a footnote he observes that Faulkner's public
statements are consistently humanist, and then he goes on
to say that "they require no dependence upon religious
assumption, but merely demonstrate a humanist confidence"
(30).

One need not go to philosophers of religion to learn what
Faulkner himself makes plain in the passage from which
Hoffman quotes in order to come to his strange conclusion.
Faulkner had said, in the passage, that his belief man will
prevail "is like the belief one has in God, Buddha, or whatever his particular abettor might be" (FN, 27). Philosophi-
cally or theologically alert humanists certainly know that
religious presuppositions are involved in their position, for
if humanism means anything at all then it means placing
man highest in one's scale of values. But Faulkner was not
satisfied even with that. It seems to me obvious that if his
humanism is *like* a belief in God or Buddha, it is not even
a secular humanism. If the terms "God" or "Buddha" have
any content at all, it is a religious content. Further, Faulkner's public statements are not so consistent as Hoffman
declares, although Faulkner has specifically identified himself as a humanist (FN, 95). Were one to read further in
the record of the seminar from which Hoffman quotes, he
would find Faulkner speaking words characteristic of a
naturalistic deism reminiscent of Thomas Paine: "To me,
a proof of God is in the firmament, the stars" (FN, 29).

We might make an end of this matter by referring to
Hyatt H. Waggoner's sensible discussion of it in Chapter
XI of his *William Faulkner: From Jefferson to the World*.
To Faulkner's definition of Christianity as "every individual's
individual code of behavior," Waggoner responds that "if
we assume that Faulkner was not deliberately pulling the
interviewer's leg with this definition, we shall have to decide

* True of so many That it can hardly be
advanced as a reason why F. is a
Xtian humanist — he may be on other grounds.

OF FAULKNER'S FICTION   19

that he was talking through his hat." He concludes that
"what Faulkner has to say, he says well only through the
symbolic language of his art. When he uses the abstract
language of philosophy and theology, his meanings are
usually vague and often apparently confused."[12]

Hoffman's error is, to use his own words, "a pardonable
mistake to make," but it does not warrant admiration. It is
a mistake theologically alert critics do not make. Lawrence
E. Bowling, for example, identifies Faulkner's humanism *
as arising from within the Christian tradition itself.[13] This
is not the whole story but it is at least a part of it. And
Ursula Brumm, who can hardly be accused of excessive
Christian piety, shows how the tradition for Faulkner always contains "at bottom . . . a guilt of rapacity and greedi-
ness which has corrupted the tradition right at its starting
point, an inevitable sin in man's civilizing efforts," and how
"history for Faulkner is really nothing but a working out of
the guilt, either by atonement, as in the case of Isaac
McCaslin, or by disasters administered as punishment."[14]
The *imitatio Christi* clearly emerging in Faulkner's later
works, she concludes, is "not the son of God or the founder
of Christianity, but Christ the archetype of man suffering,
and of those who expiate the guilt of civilization by renunciation of the power and the privilege: Quentin Compson,
Isaac McCaslin, and the Corporal" (134). One need not
agree with all Bowling and Brumm have said to see that
they are right in recognizing that Faulkner's humanism, if
it is such, involves crucial theological decisions and has deep
religious implications. The religious center in Faulkner's
fiction is quite complex, and Faulkner's public pronouncements usually mislead in this regard. *Absalom, Absalom!*

12 (Lexington: University of Kentucky Press, 1959), p. 243.
13 "Faulkner and the Theme of Innocence," *The Kenyon Review*, XX
(Summer 1958), 466-87.
14 "Wilderness and Civilization: A Note on William Faulkner," in *Three
Decades*, p. 133.

stands as a thoroughgoing critique of the tradition and of modernity from the point of view of a Christianity which owes much to Stoicism, and the very power of Isaac McCaslin's humanist solution to the problem posed by the tradition is, for Faulkner, also its piteous insufficiency.

Yet certainly one need not argue imperiously for one position. As Hoffman himself says, Faulkner is both unclear and complex. Faulkner can be read intelligently in many ways, and his ability to dramatize our perplexities from various and contradictory theological assumptions indicates his theological vitality as well as his literary versatility. Still, as the analyses offered here will show, a fairly clear theological line runs through his work from 1929 through 1942, and there is no reason to believe that it does not continue through *The Reivers.*

How, then, to talk about the Christ symbolism? For obviously it is there. Specific answers to the question can only come in the discussion of specific novels, but a general answer is clear. The Christ symbols refer beyond themselves; they are used as a part of a total fictional strategy. They may, of course, be poorly used, but in any case they never stand alone as the carrier of the novel's import. Rather, where Faulkner is most successful—as in *Light in August*—they are both supported by and contribute to the total effect. That this should be the case is reasonable in both theory and practice. This leads to the second thing of note.

Miss Brumm has hinted at it in her use of the word "archetype." I need not argue here what has so effectively been argued by Northrop Frye, C. Day Lewis, Maud Bodkin, Reed Whittemore and many others, namely, that in great literature archetypal patterns are manifestly unavoidable. This should serve to remind us that if Faulkner is tending to the business of his workshop he will inevitably strike upon generic mythic constructs of which the Christian can be considered one among others. I do not in this way mean to argue the Christian faith away as "merely a myth," but rather to point to its fundamental appeal to even the most secular mind as one total orientation or organization by which our current perplexities can be illuminated. Is it any wonder, then, that Faulkner, who is no stranger to southern Christian religiousness, should find Christian symbolism a ready and pertinent tool with which to explore his subject? Such an argument, if taken alone, is a theological cul-de-sac. But where it is supported by evidence of his signal efforts to define our perplexities in Christian terms—as in Quentin, Joe Christmas, Hightower, Sutpen, and Isaac McCaslin—and where reference is made to his repeated attempts to bring his most powerful (although perhaps insufficient) solutions to those perplexities in Christian terms—as in Dilsey, Benjy, Judith Sutpen, Lena Grove, the tall convict, Cass Edmonds, Nancy Mannigoe, the Corporal, or Charles Mallison—then the argument has both literary and theological substance.

V

It should by now be apparent that the theological naïveté too much in evidence even among those who would read Faulkner with a sympathy for his vision does not account in any important measure for the variety of critical responses to his theological center. Different theological readings are possible chiefly because of Faulkner's theological complexity. It remains for us to take a preliminary look at his theological center.

There is great significance in the fact that when Faulkner needs to explain the source of the chaos and violence in contemporary life he finds the Christian expression of man's alienation from God to be a pertinent and powerful one. By using Christian imagery he implies a Christian definition of the seriousness of man's condition. In theological terms, the ultimate meaning at stake is salvation and damnation, though one will surely want to take these terms in a highly secularized way. Yet, although Faulkner seems to find the Christian description of man's condition true, it is not at all clear that he is willing to accept the end of the Christian story as true. That man is fallen in some sense is certain; that he lives in a moral universe in which evil has real effect, in which he becomes the victim of himself, is also sure; but that God acts to redeem man is less sure. That man must work out his own salvation is probable, but that he has within him the resources which can save him is problematic.

This qualified Christian response on Faulkner's part means that we must look elsewhere for an important feature of his theological center. We are helped in such a search by Magny and Sartre, whose intelligent misreadings lead to two important considerations, both of which must be discussed at length. In the first place, we cannot accept the tacit assumption that Faulkner's vision is the same as that of his lost characters. Because it is wider and more inclusive, the metaphysics of time so unacceptable to Sartre is also not "true" finally for Faulkner. In the second place, the kind of religious meaning Faulkner's vision entails is as much Stoic as it is Christian.

Regarding Faulkner's lost characters, we should recall that the nature of the world is different as each experiencing subject apprehends it differently, and that the experiencing subject is often a composite character-author-reader. While the subject is undergoing the experience, the world as experienced must be so exclusively what it is that it cannot admit of qualification by an outside or nonexperiencing center of consciousness. Even a casual look at Faulkner's cultural materials would show how the South's historical experience affords a normative image of a fallen world, a world in which one's will meets with violent defeat. The O'Donnell-Cowley-Warren thesis points to the moral failure in the

Sartoris tradition causing the fall. For the character who cannot accept his past for what it is (Quentin, Hightower, and, to a degree, even Isaac McCaslin), the past remains as exclusive pre-emptor of his consciousness to accomplish the destruction of a meaningful present.

But by no means is Faulkner's theological vision only that of the "young aesthetes" and the "middle-aged ethicists." The assumption that it is marks the weakness of Magny's and Sartre's theses, while the discovery that it is not is the strength of Roth's. Certainly while the reader is within a lost character's sensibility, confined to his point of view, restricted to his interpretative processes, the world before him is the fallen one or the one which has failed to sustain the once operative values. Even if one establishes that the most successfully rendered characters respond to an unredeemed world while the more positive vision of other characters does not receive so convincing a rendering, still it is undeniable that the more positive vision is there. And since in a work of art one thing leads to everything else, identification of Faulkner's full vision requires an evaluation of the total structure, movement, and effect of any one work. One cannot speak of character in isolation from other elements, and certainly it is suspect to claim that any one character is speaking for Faulkner.

It is too early to admit that the more positive vision is less effectively rendered. The suggestion that it might be, however, raises a conjecture as important for theology as it is for a theological criticism of Faulkner. The problem can be pointed up by a set of related questions. Why is it that Dante's *Inferno* is a more popular text in college classrooms than his *Paradiso*? Why is Milton's *Paradise Lost* a more convincing performance than his *Paradise Regained*? Why do critics, writers, and readers in the modern period find the tragic drama or the tragic novel more emotionally moving than comedies and tend to suspect the celebrative

lyric poet of being an escapist? Religiously, why is it that
Good Friday seems more real to the modern man than Easter,
that the Crucifixion is not questioned but the Resurrection,
even when taken symbolically, is an empty metaphor?

One can respond to these questions in a variety of ways.
The tendencies indicated are perhaps the outcome of the
Protestant's breaking up of the medieval synthesis; in Protes-
tantism the solitary believer stands before the crucified Christ
without a mediating culture to sustain their relationship.
An explanation may lie in the suggestion that the rejection
of traditional embodiments of meaning has produced an
age of anxiety and meaninglessness, not because we are incapable of forming new interpretations of experience, but
because modern pluralism offers too many competing mythol-
ogies. In this case, the modern problem is the plethora and
complexity of experience rather than its emptiness. Or, perhaps Camus' essentially Stoic diagnosis of the human situation explains the matter: modern despair arises because
traditional Christianity promised too much, because in Christ
men were given a hope in excess of the facts of experience—
our despair is so deep because our hope was so high. Finally,
the questions may be investigated with two terms taken
from Christian apologetics: coherence and relevance. Coherence as the demand for integrity in man's experience
cannot be achieved where one's sensibility and intellect do
not respond in much the same way. Though one may make
a convincing intellectual argument for the presence of meaning, in the absence of a warrant from "felt life" (the phrase
is Henry James's), the intellectual argument loses relevance.

None of these answers completely explains why the
modern sensibility believes more readily in hell than in
heaven. We are left with the statistical indication that works
of despair seem to reflect the modern temper more hon-
estly than works of hope. On the basis of this phenomenon
one can account in large part for the current widespread and

favorable reception of neo-orthodoxy as a theological reflection of the modern temper. And yet, in literature, if not in theology, the fall of man involves a fortunate paradox. Where there is no evil there is no conflict, and without conflict there is no dramatic situation. Imaginative literature deals with moral problems not simply because it is a selective and interpretative account of experience, but also because its *raison d'être* lies in its presentation of conflict as a means of entertaining. The liturgical refrain of the "Exultet," "O felix culpa! quae talem et tantum meruit habere redemptorem," might also read, somewhat more prosaically, "O felix culpa! quae tales genuisse litteras meruit."

Admittedly, these are broad conjectures. If there is any truth in them at all, however, they help to tell why the literary artist of the modern period finds his work receiving a jaundiced scrutiny when his vision projects a hopeful world before the reader. They also explain why the contemporary novel must be at least modern before it can become postmodern, for once the modern vision asserts itself it can never be simply ignored. And, finally, for Christian theology these conjectures indicate that to present the Christian Gospel as merely hopeful and not also despairing may be to betray the Cross. Unless the Christian faith's whole vision of life does in fact embrace its finitude, its partiality, its sickness, Christianity cannot speak effectively to our time. Life's possibilities for damnation and real loss can be denied by Christian theology only at the risk of losing the very relevance modern literature gains by affirmation of this vision.

In the presentation of sick and driven characters, Faulkner has been able to affirm this vision convincingly because his own is wider. He sees the world as at once fallen and redeemed: he looks at one world. Because he is characteristically modern in his literary method he looks at the world through character, and at any one time it is the character's vision before the reader, or, in many cases, the vision of a composite character-author-reader. Consequently, if one is not careful to read Faulkner's works as imaginative productions, he is apt to judge Faulkner's vision as fragmentary.

The unity of Faulkner's vision does not depend upon the fact that it is, after all, one writer who is presenting various worlds. In his total theological vision, Dilsey does not live in one world and Quentin in another. Both share the same objective reality. Dilsey is not a stranger to the facts of Quentin's experience, although she does not participate in his response. Caroline Compson's querulous self-pity and Jason's cunning meanness are facts of experience to her. But Dilsey has resources the others do not tap. She observes the violence and decadence of the unredeemed world of those who have only the past as their present, but takes her own stance at the center of a redemptive present which comprehends a view of the beginning and the end.

Faulkner's ability to give a full rendering of a world at once fallen and redeemed can be seen easily by contrasting Quentin's and Dilsey's views of the Resurrection. For Quentin, Christ is an inanimate doll with "sawdust flowing from what wound in what side that not for me died not" (SF, 194). Christ does not speak to his condition. Quentin contemplates the resurrection of his body which will occur after he has carried out his plan to drown himself in the Charles River by weighting his body with some flatirons. He thinks:

> And maybe when He says Rise the eyes will come floating up too, out of the deep quiet and the sleep, to look on glory. And after awhile the flat irons would come floating up. (135)

Dilsey's vision of the power and the glory is generically different. In church during Shegog's Easter sermon, "Dilsey sat bolt upright . . . crying rigidly and quietly in the annealment and the blood of the remembered Lamb" (313). As

she leaves church, she is able to place the Compson history
in the comprehensive context of a Christian view of time:

> "I've seed de first en de last," Dilsey said. . . .
> "First en last whut?" Frony said.
> "Never you mind," Dilsey said. "I seed de beginnin, en now
> I sees de endin." (313)

VI

　　　Dilsey furnishes an easy case for the positive content
of the Christian faith even as Quentin exhibits the despair
familiar to its pessimistic side. But the Christian faith does
not provide the only frame of reference in terms of which
Faulkner renders positive and negative responses to modern
experience.

　　We should not dwell upon the fallen character of Faulkner's world in the second place, then, because the meaning
and truth of his religious center is as much Stoic as it is
Christian. To interpret his vision as simply skeptical is to
diagnose the symptom as the disease. Faulkner's religious
center, as revealed by his entire imaginative performance—
theme, character, action, the total structure of his individual
fictions—is best described as a tension between Stoic and
Christian visions. The tension is not a dualism, not mere
strain, not a contradiction. His is a religious center of tension.
This is another way of describing the unity of his theological
core; the world in Christian terms is at once fallen and redeemed, and in Stoic terms it is hostile, inhuman, thought-
less, alien, and hopeless on the one hand and the locus of
possible human meaning on the other. Except for a few instances, the theological assumptions (unarticulated and for
the most part unknown) underlying his characters' vision—
negative or positive—can be identified as either Stoic or
Christian.

One may, of course, take this central theological tension as evidence of an irresolution on Faulkner's part: he is trying to have it both ways. But such a conclusion assumes Faulkner to be engaged directly in a theological task in which he has attempted but failed to reach a resolution. If we assume Faulkner's task to be primarily aesthetic and judge by the mimetic achievement of his fiction, we can at the most only claim that he has given lyrical validity to both alternatives, that he is able *where the fictive logic demands it* to make each aesthetically valid.

Because the history of Christian thought is so complex, so eclectic, there is not a thoroughgoing difference between orthodox Christianity and classical Stoicism. Stoic rationalism, especially in the doctrine of the Logos, contributed to the Christian understanding of the relation of God to nature; the Stoic emphasis upon human brotherhood and the attendant imperative upon duty became part of the Christian ethic. And Stoicism itself is not single and unambiguous; it has its own phases, its own sidelines of thought, and its own inner contradictions, and its modern expressions do not derive in a clear line from its classical forms. Nevertheless, as Paul Tillich documents so well in *The Courage to Be,* Stoic religiousness is fundamentally different from the Christian and is, in fact, the classical religious alternative to it.[15] For example, in the realm of ethics, in which the valuation of a human act is considered, the notion that human brotherhood roots in love is definitely antithetical to the Stoic doctrine of *eudaimonia,* tranquility. Edwyn Bevan's classic study of Stoicism makes clear that the Stoic "was not to *concern* himself with his brethren . . . he was only to serve them."[16] Bevan sees a central difference between Stoicism and Christianity to lie in their incompatible ideals of Detachment and Love:

The Stoics, I think, saw with perfect truth that if you were

---

15 (New Haven: Yale University Press, 1952), p. 9.
16 *Stoics and Sceptics* (New York: Barnes & Noble, Inc., 1959), p. 66.

going to allow any least entrance of love and pity into the breast, you admitted something whose measure you could not control, and might just as well give up the idea of inner tranquillity at once. Where love is, action cannot be without desire; the action of love has eminently regard to fruit, in the sense of some result beyond itself—the one thing that seems to matter is whether the loved person really is helped by your action. Of course you run the risk of frustrated desire and disappointment. The Stoic sage was never frustrated and never disappointed. Gethsemane, looked at from his point of view, was a signal break-down. The Christian's Ideal Figure could never be accepted by the Stoic as an example of his typical Wise Man. (70)

In the realm of metaphysics or ontology, especially that area of it which verges upon a theological doctrine of man, there is also a fundamental difference between the Stoic and the Christian. The Stoic doctrine of man, which identifies man's reason, his ruling principle, as a detached spark of the Divine Reason, could not admit the notion of guilt or guilty existence. The concept of guilt would contradict the rationality of man, disallow his essential identity with the Divine, the Universal, the Natural. Yet, though guilt or guilty existence is a concept alien to the Stoic mind, evil is not. The undeniable presence of evil in experience can be explained only as a defection of reason and will or as dire fate. The proper response to it is courageous resignation, assent. A modern Stoic, Bertrand Russell, has described the Stoic vision and the strategy of Stoic courage: "only on the firm foundation of unyielding despair, can the soul's habitation . . . be safely built."[17] For him,

> to defy with Promethean constancy a hostile universe, to keep its evil always in view, always actively hated, to refuse no pain that the malice of Power can invent, appears to be the duty of all who will not bow before the inevitable. . . . there is a kind of

[17] "A Free Man's Worship," *Mysticism and Logic* (Garden City, New York: Doubleday Anchor Books, 1957), pp. 45-46.

self-assertion which it is necessary for the wise to overcome. . . .
the Stoic freedom in which wisdom consists is found in the
submission of our desires, but not of our thoughts. From the
submission of our desires springs the virtue of resignation. . . .
Freedom comes only to those who no longer ask of life that it
shall yield them any of those personal goods that are subject to
the mutations of Time. (48-49)

In his essay *On Providence,* Seneca encourages his friend
Lucilius to bear evil and bad fortune with fortitude because
"in this you may outstrip God; he is exempt from enduring
evil, while you are superior to it" (VI. 6).[18] As C. M. Bowra
puts it, "in their divine security [the gods] . . . lack something of the dignity which man gains from the short time
at his disposal."[19] The ideal Stoic does suffer, says Seneca:
"I do not mean to say that the brave man is insensible to
these [externals which cause suffering], but that he over-
comes them" (*On Providence,* II. 2); yet, he is able to endure because in the most dire fate "it is nothing of our own
that perishes" (*On Providence,* V. 8). What is "our own,"
he tells Lucilius in his letter "On the Happy Life," is our
soul, our rational being derived from divine reason, which
provides the good (Stoic) man with "peace of mind, and
lasting tranquillity" (*Epistles,* XCII. 2, 3). Neither suffering
nor death can reach the soul, one's rational being: Anytus
and Meletus, Epictetus likes to repeat, can kill Socrates, but
they cannot harm him.

The Stoic's refusal to recognize guilt dictates that his
adjustment to experience be one of active renunciation.
He affirms himself in the face of fate and death and sickness.

---

[18] Quotations from Seneca's *On Providence* are from the Loeb Classical
Library edition of *Moral Essays,* I, trans. John W. Basore (Cambridge, Mass.:
Harvard University Press, 1958). The quotation from Seneca's *Epistles* is
taken from the Loeb edition of *Ad Lucilium Epistulae Morales,* II, trans.
Richard M. Gummere (Cambridge, Mass.: Harvard University Press, 1953).

[19] *The Greek Experience* (Cleveland: The World Publishing Co., 1957),
p. 53.

"It is the part of courage, when misfortune comes, to bear without repining the ruin of our hopes," says Russell (49-50), and Seneca and Epictetus, like Camus, would add that one does not fear if one does not hope. But the vision of a world fallen "from essential rationality to existential foolishness as a matter of responsibility and as a problem of guilt," is foreign to the Stoic; it could not be otherwise, says Tillich, "for the courage to face one's own guilt leads to the question of salvation instead of renunciation."[20] Human failure in Stoicism is a failure of nerve, an error in judgment, or a result of ignorance rather than sin; it is a failure because of finitude rather than guilt. Like Kierkegaard's "knight of infinite renunciation," the Stoic responds to the human condition by heroic or courageous resignation. By virtue of his will, a surrogate for faith, he is capable of a complete renunciation of all that is not soul. He "can become a tragic hero by his own powers" because he can will to act in harmony with a universal principle.[21] This means that he can therefore "rejoice in the security of the universal" (86), says Kierkegaard, and find the peace it provides. The Stoic thus by his own act of will and reason puts meaning into experience, manufactures a truth which is *there* only so long as it receives his assent.

The Christian's diagnosis of the human problem in terms of sin and guilt means that the solution must come by a reconciliation with the God from whom man is estranged. Sin, as the condition of existence, means that man's very will and reason—so crucial in the Stoic scheme of "salvation by acquiescence," an act of the will in harmony with reason—are unable to save him for they *are* the problem. The Christian claims to have discovered meaning *in* reality, a God-

20 *The Courage to Be*, p. 17.

21 Søren Kierkegaard, *Fear and Trembling and Sickness Unto Death*, trans. Walter Lowrie (Garden City, New York: Doubleday Anchor Books, 1954), p. 77.

given and guaranteed meaning always there and available to him who will receive it in humility. Stoic courage is heroic, while Christian courage is humble; Stoic endurance is a human achievement, while Christian endurance is a gift of forgiving love.

The touchstone for judging the *kind* of religious meaning in Faulkner's vision is his understanding of the origin and nature of evil and the resources for dealing with it. Specifically, this question is raised by asking what went wrong with the tradition. Where is it, or why is it, that the Sartorises failed? Was their failure a result of a wrong assessment of the nature of things, or was it a failure of nerve? How is man to live in the face of all the violence, chaos, and decadence so apparent in modern experience? The question for theological anthropology is whether man's basic problem is finitude or sin and the related question for soteriology is how, qua human and only finite or qua human and guilty before his creator, the resources for overcoming evil or sin are made available. Finally, the question can be raised another way: do Faulkner's bedrock virtues of courage, endurance, pride, and love ultimately have a Christian or a Stoic reference?

Answers to these questions can be found only in an analysis of the texts before us, and I have possibly already said too much. For the present, I need make only two further observations. In the first place, it is apparent that the more comprehensive vision—be it Christian or Stoic—of a Dilsey must be thought of as closely representative of Faulkner's vision. The perception involved is like a one-way street. Faulkner can see what a Dilsey can see and Dilsey can see what a Quentin can see, but Quentin cannot share Dilsey's vision—he is too preoccupied in looking back.

In the second place, it is apparent that Faulkner's religious center has from the beginning been more complex, his private vision has been more constant, than those who emphasize his pilgrimage would imply. The Stoic and Christian assessments, with him from the beginning, have formed the poles of a theological tension. If they saw anything religious at all in Faulkner, the early critics could see little else beside his Stoicism. But we do not have to wait until the appearance of *Go Down, Moses,* in 1942, in order to find a balance between the visions of a fallen world and a redeemed world. *The Sound and the Fury* of 1929 is a celebration of Easter's victory as well as a rendering of Good Friday's despair; it is an aesthetic demonstration that man can live meaningfully in the midst of a hopeless condition. In what is often called his most skeptical period, Faulkner is capable of a Benjy, a Dilsey, an Addie Bundren, or a Lena Grove. For this reason, I would claim that Faulkner's religious center has not undergone any fundamental change.

The Sound and the Fury:
The Locus and Status of Meaning

I

BEFORE the publication of *The Sound and the Fury* on October 7, 1929, the general public had seen from the pen of William Faulkner only some poor lost generation poetry and three novels, *Soldiers' Pay* (1926), *Mosquitoes* (1927) and *Sartoris* (January 31, 1929). In retrospect it is easy to find signs of what was to come. The scene of David and Patricia's escape through the swamp in *Mosquitoes,* for example, contains elements of Faulkner at his full power. But that is in retrospect, and one surely could not have expected the discipline of characterization to say nothing of the apparent recklessness of technique which must have struck early readers of *The Sound and the Fury.* Of course, Faulkner had written *Sanctuary* earlier, but he was to revise it before its publication in 1931, so even the discipline of that book was absent from the public eye.

Very early estimates of *The Sound and the Fury* criticized little other than the technique, and at the close of the Faulkner corpus with *The Reivers* (1962) it still stands as Faulkner's most ambitious experiment in the art of the novel. It is the one he anguished over the most, he repeatedly said, and often he spoke of it as his "finest" or "most magnificent failure" (*FN,* 9; *FU,* 61, 77). If, as he also frequently said, greatness should be measured by the scope of a writer's attempt, it is not surprising that he felt *The Sound and the*

35

Fury to be his most important novel, for the theological
depth of the whole performance is commensurate with and
in large measure inseparable from his celebrated technique.
Whether or not its theological depth could have been attained in another way, less demanding of the reader, is
beside the point. The fact is that in this book, put together
in this way, Faulkner has achieved an aesthetically ordered
and searching exploration of some crucial theological issues.

Because Benjy's section opens the novel, the reader is initially confined to the point of view of an idiot, since this
third son of Caroline and Jason Compson III has the mentality of a three-year-old, or, as one of the Negroes puts it,
"he been three years old thirty years" (*SF,* 36). Of course,
Benjy's section does not give an actual reproduction of his
mental processes; rather, an illusion of verisimilitude is
created dramatically by the objectification in language of his
interior life. By skillful use of the interior monologue,
Faulkner makes an idiot's center of consciousness the most
reliable of the three first-person narrations in the book.[1]
Though Benjy introduces fragments of Compson history from
his earliest memories in 1898 to the present (April 7, 1928),
most of his monologue concerns the period between 1898
and 1910, the latter being the year of Caddy's marriage
(April 25) as well as of Quentin's suicide (June 2). It is
of Caddy's presence that Benjy is most fond. That he thinks
of her so often in these pages is made credible by his being
reminded of her name by the golfers' shouting for their
caddies in the pasture, now a golf course, adjoining the

---

[1] There are several ways of classifying the various levels of writing in
the stream-of-consciousness technique. The scheme used here is the one
given in Frederick J. Hoffman's *Freudianism and the Literary Mind,* 2nd ed.
(Baton Rouge: Louisiana State University Press, 1957), pp. 128-30: (1) the
traditional, (2) the level of the preconscious or of conscious revery, (3) the
level of the subconscious, and (4) the level of the unconscious. Another
useful method can be found in Lawrence E. Bowling's "What is the Stream
of Consciousness Technique?" *PMLA,* LXV (June 1950), 333-45.

Compson place. This pasture, called by Quentin and Caddy "Benjy's pasture," was sold to provide funds to send Quentin to Harvard and to pay for Caddy's wedding. And, by far the major portion of Benjy's attention to events between 1898 and 1910 is concentrated on some events of the day Damuddy (the grandmother) died in 1898, and of the day his name was changed from Maury to Benjamin in 1900.

All of Benjy's section is given in the past tense. By the use of italics, the reader is initially made aware of time shifts in Benjy's thinking. But the logic of the shifts is maintained internally; the italics make typographically apparent what can be discerned by noting the juxtaposed images or emotional situations in two successive scenes. Benjy seems to range over the thirty years of his rememberable past without discrimination. Time shifts do not always occur from present to past and back to present. Rather, shifts in time can be from any past or present scene to another. Benjy's range of attention is only apparently indiscriminate, for when one has finished his section, the crucial events of the novel are before him. What one learns later about an event or a scene by the narration in Quentin's or Jason's section is often less objective than what one learns from Benjy, although Benjy is an idiot.

Quentin's section opens with traditional language, but at points and moments his monologue is at the level of the subconscious; that is, willful control of his conscious mind is, for the most part, absent. The reader's focus is upon Quentin himself, upon his organization of and reaction to events. In Benjy's section, the interior monologue is never obviously interpretative, except once, when Benjy says "even Jason was through eating" (46), but Quentin's section is all interpretation, sometimes by logical, normal syntactical language of the traditional stream-of-consciousness type, sometimes by conscious revery, sometimes by a linguistic rendering of the subconscious.

In Benjy's consciousness, the past is no less vivid than the present; indeed, the distinction between time past and time present is simply not a part of his mentality, except to the extent that he can maintain in his memory a short sequence of events. One can say that Benjy is completely time bound and yet free of time altogether. Unaware of time's movement, he is conscious always of its undifferentiated presence in the full immediacy of events; yet because its presence is undifferentiated, he is completely incapable of abstracting it as a quality of events. The term "time shift" is applicable only to the reader's experience and not to Benjy's. Faulkner reinforces this phenomenon by uniform punctuation and capitalization (except for the italics) throughout the section.

For Quentin, however, time definitely exists as something to be measured. The ticking off of mechanical time by his watch haunts him, and time is the context in which he defines his major problem. Time shifts occurring in his section are indicated by several devices, including the use of italics and the lack of normal punctuation and capitalization. Quentin, of course, concentrates in his memory on the same period as Benjy, but chiefly on those events of the period revealing his distraction about Caddy's gradual sexual corruption: the scene in 1898 in which Caddy, age seven, takes off her dress to play in the branch and gets her drawers muddy; Caddy's various meetings with Dalton Ames and her marriage to Herbert Head; his own attempt with Caddy to carry out a suicide compact; and his conversations with his father about Caddy's promiscuity and his own guilt. In his section, much new material about the Compson past is added, and some of the scenes remembered in Benjy's section are clarified and placed in sequence.

Jason's section is chiefly conscious revery. Compared with Benjy's and Quentin's, his mind appears sane, normal, and rational. Although his monologue shows no loss of willful control, it has the great fluidity of a daydream. He too dips

in and out of the past as he recounts self-righteously the
events of his vicious and deceitful dealings with Miss Quentin, his niece, on April 6, 1928. Time for him is also mechanical and hostile; it is that realm of experience in which he
frantically pursues his material values, and for this pursuit
there is never enough time.

The narrative device employed in the fourth section requires no extended comment since it approximates the usual
third-person, objective author narration. One can say, however, that the stream-of-consciousness framework is not completely abandoned since, with two exceptions, we watch the
events of this Easter Day in the dominating presence of
Dilsey. It might be well also to indicate generally the concept of time involved in this section, for if the narrative
technique is not radically different here (since the progression of narrative technique from Benjy's through Dilsey's
sections is one of gradual objectification), the concept of
time is. There are no flashbacks; no juggling of chronology
occurs. Rather, events are described as they occur, taken as
they come, lived through by Dilsey as they happen. The
author's objective stance, his timeless vantage point, casts
a feel of eternalness about this section, not in such a way
as to negate time, but to fulfill it. This is reinforced by the
dominant theme of the section, presented symbolically in
the figure of Dilsey, who does not retreat from time as
Quentin does or frantically try to beat it as Jason does but
accepts it as the context in which she endures—"I seed de
beginnin, en now I sees de endin"—and experiences "de
power en de glory" (313).

II

The formal division of the novel into four sections,
differentiated by focus of narration and narrative technique

as well as by the implied concepts of time, provides one way of seeing the relationship of its parts. A division more useful for a theological analysis is possible if attention is given to the thematic value of the action represented in the novel. In this case, the novel's action can be seen as having a beginning, middle, and end—that is, the aesthetically complete and logically credible causal relationships of plot. But since the thirty years of Compson history covered in this book are not given in normal chronology, since, indeed, the first three sections recapitulate many of the same events, the beginning, middle, and end of the plot do not function to create the usual suspense—that is, an uncertainty about the outcome of events. Rather, suspense is chiefly that of theme: anxious uncertainty centers upon meaning, and the meaning both of particular events and of their causal relationships is known only at the very end of the book when the major themes have been rendered by the completion of character.

Two major themes run at counterpoint throughout *The Sound and the Fury,* qualifying and deepening one another, neither emerging as unambiguously dominant and neither mitigated for the sake of the other. Their juxtaposition gives the novel its theological significance, and their successful exemplification in the unity of symbol and action gives the novel its artistic power. Both themes refer finally to the status of meaning in modern experience: the first to its negative status, loss and absence; the second to its positive status, presence and endurance.

Yet the organization of the novel's plot of thematic suspense, rendered through character and exemplified in symbol and action, is even more complex than has been indicated. Although the reader does sense that Quentin's suicide is a denouement, he is not certain of its logical position in the plot because the front stage or present-tense action occurs eighteen years later and finds its own denouement in Jason's

attempt to recover his lost hoard. Faulkner has really presented two major actions: the first of Quentin's relationship
with Caddy and his father, ending in his suicide and Caddy's
leaving home; and the second of Jason and Miss Quentin,
ending in his frustration and her disappearance.

These two actions do not stand to each other as major
and minor plot but are embodiments of the two sides of
the first theme. The Quentin–Caddy–Mr. Compson line of
action embodies the theme of the *loss* of meaning. The
dominant emphasis is not simply that meaning is absent,
but that it was once and is no longer present. The Jason–
Miss Quentin line of action ironically embodies the theme
of the *absence* of meaning. There is no problem here of the
loss of meaning since there is no acknowledgment that traditional interpretations of experience ever did have validity
or that they pose any problem for the present. The irony lies
in the fact that the meaning assumed to be present is so
shallow it does not provide a genuine or acceptable alternative to the meaning Quentin feels to be lost. The second
theme—the presence or endurance of meaning—emerges
from the refraction of the two major lines of action through
the characters of Benjy and Dilsey. In both actions Benjy
and Dilsey are involved, not as causal agents but as refrac-
ting agents through whom the actions appear as theme symbolically embodied in their characters. The refraction of the
Quentin–Caddy–Mr. Compson action through the character
of Benjy (he is chiefly concerned with this action) gives
rise to the theme of the *presence* of meaning. The refraction
of the Jason–Miss Quentin action through the character of
Dilsey (her section has to do almost solely with this action)
gives rise to the theme of the *endurance* of meaning.

The first theme dominates Quentin's and Jason's sections;
the second generally characterizes Benjy's section but is
developed especially in Dilsey's. Just as the first theme is

in general developed literally in the midst of the second, so the second theme in its general development passes through and encompasses those sections where the first theme is felt. Of course, the themes are not sharply separable according to section. Benjy's section introduces both themes without giving focus to either. Quentin strives to establish the reality of the second but succeeds only in affirming the first. Though he assumes the reality of the second theme, Jason, too, by the dramatic irony of his section, affirms the negative status of meaning. Dilsey's section brings both themes into focus, and the second emerges as dominant.

The novel's lack of surface form is related to the thematic organization of its plot. We enter through the mind of an idiot on his birthday. Then we are taken back eighteen years with Quentin on the day of his suicide. In the next section, Jason introduces us to the Snopes world of rationalization on the day prior to Benjy's birthday. Finally, we are outside the mind of any of the characters and follow Dilsey on Easter Sunday, the day following Benjy's birthday. On an initial level, the novel's shapelessness is a function of its first basic theme, the loss of significant shape to experience: the characteristic shape is no shape at all. A closer reading, however, shows shapelessness to be only apparent and not actual. The novel moves from Benjy's minimally interpreted and apparently chaotic world, to Quentin's overinterpreted but apparently empty world, through the "sane" and rationalized world in which Jason lives, and ends in a solid world of enduring values where Dilsey finds "de power en de glory." On a more subtle level, the second theme emerges: experience is also seen to have a truly redemptive structure.

So it is that both themes pervade the novel's total movement. The novel gains unusual power from the fact that the themes rendered by the actions and their refractions are expressed also in the symbolism. The novel's thematic power is a function of the achieved unity of symbol and action.

III

Within the novel itself, the Quentin–Caddy–Mr. Compson action is confined to a twelve-year period, but it draws upon a rich and complex antecedent situation. Quentin's suicide stems from his inability to come to terms with his situation, with the set of historical conditions to which he is peculiarly sensitive and in the face of which he is pathetically ineffectual. Full details of the situation antecedent to the novel are not given in the novel itself, yet they are available in the Appendix, a history of the Compsons from 1699 to 1945, published in 1946 and expanding the family history backward and forward in time.

The Appendix demands close attention for two reasons. In the first place, it raises the problem of how Faulkner's writings are to be viewed, whether he is primarily a novelist at all, or whether he is, instead, a builder of legend or a writer of epic. If he is a novelist, then the Appendix should not be necessary for an understanding of the book; or if it is necessary, and Faulkner is a novelist, then he is a novelist of a special kind which we must define. If the Appendix is not necessary for an understanding of the novel, then just what is its relationship to the novel and what is its status in the Faulkner corpus? These questions are dealt with most easily by giving attention first to the other reason why the Appendix demands scrutiny: it does tell us something about the heritage of the Compsons, and this heritage constitutes the initial situation of the Quentin–Caddy–Mr. Compson line of action.

Faulkner begins the history with the Indian Ikkemotubbe from whom, in 1813, Jason Lycurgus Compson I obtained the square mile of land located in the center of what was to be Jefferson. The land was sold piecemeal until in 1910 only the house and adjoining garden, stables, and servants'

cabins were left, and in 1933 that too was sold by Jason IV.[2]
Ikkemotubbe, being "a man of wit and imagination as well
as a shrewd judge of character, including his own" (3),
corrupted the French translation of his Indian name, "The
Man," into "Doom." Although he is not a Compson, he is
involved in their history, a history which seems to be one of
doom, of inevitable failure, of lost causes.

The earliest Compson, Quentin MacLachan, fled from
Scotland to Carolina after having failed in the rebellion of
Charles Edward against George II in 1746 at Culloden. He
fled again, to Kentucky, at the outbreak of the American
Revolution. His son, Charles Stuart, "fled by night, running
true to family tradition" (5), after the failure of a plot to
secede the Mississippi Valley from the United States. Jason I
and his son, Governor Quentin MacLachan, seem to have
enjoyed some good fortune. All the Compsons were gamblers "provided the gambit was desperate and the odds long
enough" (5), and the Governor is described as "the last
Compson who would not fail at everything he touched save
longevity or suicide" (7). Jason II, a southern general, who
in his old age was "a sort of privileged pseudo-Daniel Boone-
Robinson Crusoe, who had not returned to juvenility because
actually he had never left it" (8), failed in two major Civil
War battles. His son, Jason III, the father in *The Sound
and the Fury,* a frustrated classicist, lived out his life "with
a decanter of whiskey and a litter of dogeared Horaces and
Livys and Catulluses" (8).

In *Sartoris* Faulkner deals with another old aristocratic
family of his imaginary country, but there is a marked difference in the way he handles the tradition in this earlier
novel. The very name of Sartoris evokes an atmosphere of
death and fatality:

The music went on in the dusk softly; the dusk was peopled

2 *The Mansion,* pp. 322-25, gives another account of the property's
history.

with ghosts of glamorous and old disastrous things. And if they were just glamorous enough, there was sure to be a Sartoris in them, and then they were sure to be disastrous. Pawns. But the Player, and the game He plays . . . He must have a name for His pawns, though. But perhaps Sartoris is the game itself—a game outmoded and played with pawns shaped too late and to an old dead pattern, and of which the Player Himself is a little wearied. For there is death in the sound of it, and a glamorous fatality, like silver pennons downrushing at sunset, or a dying fall of horns along the road to Roncevaux. (380, ellipsis in the original)

To the Sartorises Faulkner devoted another book, *The Unvanquished*, a collection of related episodes told from the point of view of young Bayard Sartoris. This is the only example in Faulkner's work of a fairly sustained and direct look at an aristocratic figure of the Civil War period. As its title indicates, *The Unvanquished* is an elegiac tribute to the glorious, dead southern past, especially to the book's central figure, Colonel John Sartoris.

Faulkner's treatment of the Compsons contrasts significantly with his treatment of the Sartorises. The Compson past in *The Sound and the Fury* is seen as interpreted in the present by Quentin and his father. Even the Appendix, a direct treatment of the Compsons, in one place grouped with the Sartorises, is markedly more objective than Faulkner's earlier treatment of the Sartorises. Faulkner the man is supposedly closer to his materials when dealing with the Sartorises since John Sartoris appears to be modeled after Faulkner's great-grandfather, Col. William C. Falkner, soldier, railroad builder, legislator, and author of several books, including a best-seller, *The White Rose of Memphis* (1881). But Faulkner's novels testify that as he moves further into the present he is less likely to indulge in a moon-and-magnolia picture of the southern past. This would indicate that his chief interest is not in the past for its own sake but as it is formative of the present and as it functions symbolically to illuminate the present. When Faulkner treats the past directly he is more likely to be sentimental than when he is subject to the discipline of seeing modern problems in terms of it.

The Appendix tells us that the Compson past, for all the doom and defeat to be found there, contains something of real worth, embodies a "truth" which is still of value. It is a history of decay and degeneration, indicating negatively if in no other way that there was a time when men were secure in a trust in their own humanity. This is made especially clear when, in comparison with the Sartorises and the Compsons, the Snopeses are identified as "inexplicable yet quite predictable in that they were in no sense whatever to be trusted" (*SF*, 17). Summing up the family history, Faulkner says that in Jason IV, "the childless bachelor,"

> ended that long line of men who had had something in them of decency and pride even after they had begun to fail at the integrity and the pride had become mostly vanity and selfpity: from the expatriate who had to flee his native land with little else except his life yet who still refused to accept defeat, through the man who gambled his life and his good name twice and lost twice and declined to accept that either, and the one who with only a clever small quarterhorse for tool avenged his dispossessed father and grandfather and gained a principality, and the brilliant and gallant governor and the general who though he failed at leading in battle brave and gallant men at least risked his own life too in the failing, to the cultured dipsomaniac who sold the last of his patrimony not to buy drink but to give one of his descendants at least the best chance in life he could think of. (13)

Faulkner is not easy upon the tradition in this Appendix, for the Compsons are a "rotting family" in a "rotting house" (17). It is clear that he questions the traditional values and meanings, but it is equally clear that he is attracted by the

scope of the tradition's failure as well as by the largeness of
its attempt to define, in an essentially Stoic manner, a world
of stable meanings. In an interview, Faulkner, confronted
with the fact that more of his characters go down than survive, is reported to have carried on the following exchange:

> WF: That's all right. That they go down doesn't matter. It's
> *how* they go under.
> INT: And what is the way to go under?
> WF: It's to go under when trying to do more than you know
> how to do. It's trying to defy defeat even if it's inevitable.[3]

What we learn of the Compsons here is some detail of how
they go under. The earlier Compsons went under well
(Stoically); the later ones, except perhaps for Caddy, the
impulsive free spirit, "ageless and beautiful, cold serene and
damned" (12), did not go under well at all.

If, then, the Appendix gives us reliable information about
Faulkner's attitude toward the southern tradition, is it really
a necessary part of the novel to which seventeen years later
it was appended? If one is trying to determine what Faulkner
himself believes, then this history (which, after all, is still
fiction and must be read that way) is of value, since here
Faulkner's own voice is less disguised than in his novels. In
this case, the Appendix stands as Faulkner's later judgment
upon his characters, and it is remarkable that the material
and mental and biological degeneration of the Compsons,
so much the subject matter of the novel, becomes, in Faulkner's own reading, important as an index of moral decay.

The Appendix can lead one into the novel, can give
Faulkner's reading of what he has dramatized, but is it
therefore necessary for the novel's integrity as an aesthetic
whole? If the novel achieves what Faulkner has virtually
said he wanted it to achieve, then the Appendix stands only

---

[3] Cynthia Grenier, "The Art of Fiction: An Interview with William
Faulkner—September, 1955," *Accent*, XVI (Summer 1956), 172

as a document between the Yoknapatawpha County legend and the novel which draws from that legend. It is possible that Faulkner's later statement about what he tried to do in the novel is false, or it is possible that his achievement is something other than what he felt it to be. Certainly if the latter is the case, it is what he actually achieved that must be judged. But a careful reading of the novel gives no reason to depart from Faulkner's virtual statement of his intentions. Faulkner can be regarded as engaged in a "double labor": he is a novelist in the strict sense of the word, but he is also, as Cowley has said, a builder of legend, and the novels participate in a wider fiction than their own.[4] It is then legitimate to characterize his "world" and to speak of his "total vision."

In the novel there is a real beginning, complete in itself. Although the Compson history is not given in detail, the initial situation of the novel's action gives ample reference to the family inheritance by the symbolic use of character. Quentin's initial condition, his *donnée,* is a conjunction of his character and the historical circumstances of the family. Important in the novel is not the specific detail of the early Compson history; rather, it is Quentin's reaction to that history, especially to the values for which in his own mind the family stood. Nor is there in the Jason–Miss Quentin line of action any need for more detailed reference to Compson history, although some information is given when Jason makes fun of the family's self-image. If anyone, it is Dilsey who has a great concrete sense of the past. Benjy, of course, is incapable, except by way of report of the words of others, of making any reference to details of family history.

So it is that the historical information given in the Appendix is of interest chiefly in the Yoknapatawpha legend and not crucial to the novel itself. In other words, the Appendix contributes to the larger task Faulkner has set for himself. We should not, however, think of the Yoknapa-

---

[4] "Introduction to *The Portable Faulkner,*" in *Three Decades,* p. 94.

tawpha legend as a giant novel built of the individual works. The legend emerges only through the individual novels and stories—and the various items (maps, genealogies, chronologies, family histories, author's notes) accompanying them. It functions as an economic device by which Faulkner can draw upon, in any specific work, all that he has accomplished in other works. As he put it himself when asked to explain the origin of the legend, "I was still trying to reduce my one individual experience of the world into one compact thing which could be picked up and held in the hands at one time" (FN, 81).

The lines of dramatic action in the novel are independent of the Appendix, but they draw from it a depth of reference which enhances the rich experience already afforded by the novel. The mere presence of the Appendix shows that Faulkner continued to be concerned with the themes and issues of the story, that many years after its publication he still had a sense of the importance of its themes and perhaps also a sense that he had failed to convey all he wanted by the novel. Among other things, this shows that Faulkner had not, by 1946 at least, abandoned his earlier theological interests, though certainly he had adopted other techniques, strategies, and details with which to explore them.

IV

Quentin provides the focus of character for the first line of action. The reader comes to his section having already had the experience of Benjy's faithful reports. When Quentin's monologue reaches the level of the subconscious, the reader is therefore not utterly confused. What one does discover in Quentin's section is how his particular sensibility leads him to the point of suicide.

Quentin asks of life that it be meaningful in a certain way, namely that it support what he takes to be the traditional criterion of meaning. His inflexibility, his rigidity, on the point of what meaning must look like, is commensurate with his "presbyterian" (9) temperament and is part of the givenness of his character. Essentially he is a Stoic rationalist and a puritan moralist. Not only in his own section but also in Benjy's, he is shown constantly interpreting the events of the Compson household in moralistic terms. His understanding of the tradition is purely moralistic and intellectual. He does not participate in its spirit, but has learned its forms, interpreting them with a legalistic rigidity which precludes his bending to present experience and presages his breaking against it.

As he develops his various strategies for dealing with present experience, he undergoes an intellectualization of his problem. He moves from an attention to sex to a concern with being itself. His initial definition of his problem in terms of sex stems from his puritan moralism turning in upon itself. He is literally sick with sex, can see Caddy only as a sex abstraction and not as a person, only as the weak custodian of a virginity embodying the family honor. He is incapable of love (there is a hint that he may be physically impotent) but capable of intellectual incest. He is, finally, capable only of self-love. In a singularly fine monograph on *The Sound and the Fury,* Peter Swiggart has defined the character of Quentin's sex obsession clearly. "His incestuous aims," says Swiggart, "are egocentric in origin and mental in character. They exemplify his moral perversion and lack of true affection for the sister with whom he is so morally concerned. She becomes, for him, only an ego-projection of his own rational fury; and his moral condemnations reflect back upon himself. Incestuous desire, for Quentin, is only a narcissistic wish for moral auto-eroticism."[5]

---

[5] Peter Swiggart, "Moral and Temporal Order in *The Sound and the Fury," The Sewanee Review,* LXI (Spring 1953), 225.

Quentin's sensibility, thus constituted, provides Faulkner with a sensitive consciousness with which to explore the tradition both in its own terms and as it might function to identify a resource for meaning in modern experience. Faulkner can do this because he places Quentin's narrative point of view at the moment of his suicide, at the point where his entire progression of character comes up for review by an ingenious but blind rationalism. Ironically, Quentin's narrative stance allows him too, like Dilsey, to see the beginning and the end, but unlike Dilsey he is, even at the point of suicide, still trapped in mechanical time.

For all the apparent disorganization of his section, it is possible to discern three major phases through which his character has progressed: an initial focus upon Caddy's sexual behavior as the test of the tradition's validity in the present; a shift in focus from ethics to metaphysics, from sex to time as his private problem, with the added attempt here to bring sex and time together; and, finally, a capitulation to his father's nihilism, a concern with being itself, with death as a means of avoiding the meaninglessness of time by referring his problem to eternity. At the point of his narration, Quentin has just completed the last phase. He therefore speaks in the past tense of all three phases, and about the first two he speaks in the light of the final perspective of the third.

These three phases can be abstracted from Faulkner's account of Quentin in the Appendix. Faulkner begins by speaking of the relationship in Quentin's mind between the tradition and Caddy's sexuality:

> Who loved not his sister's body but some concept of Compson honor precariously and (he knew well) only temporarily supported by the minute fragile membrane of her maidenhead as a miniature replica of all the whole vast globy earth may be poised on the nose of a trained seal. (9)

Quentin's intellectual entertainment of the idea of incest

emerges in the second phase as a partial surrender of the traditional Stoic frame of reference and an attempt to redeem time (the past) by an ego-centered inversion of his puritan moralism:

> Who loved not the idea of the incest which he would not commit, but some presbyterian concept of its eternal punishment: he, not God, could by that means cast himself and his sister both into hell, where he could guard her forever and keep her forevermore intact amid the eternal fires. (9)

Finally, Quentin's third phase completes his renunciation of Stoic rationalism and finds him fearful of losing all meaning in time. His self-love culminates in a psychoneurotic death plunge:

> But who loved death above all, who loved only death, loved and lived in a deliberate and almost perverted anticipation of death as a lover loves and deliberately refrains from the waiting willing friendly tender incredible body of his beloved, until he can no longer bear not the refraining but the restraint and so flings, hurls himself, relinquishing, drowning. (9-10)

This outline of Quentin's progression of character is supported by the dramatic movement of the novel itself. In the initial phase, his focus is upon inherited forms of honorable behavior, and his specific attention is upon Caddy's sexual behavior. Throughout his life, Quentin is sensitive to incidents violating the forms of traditional morality. In the earliest scene of the novel, the nine-year-old Quentin threatens Caddy if she takes off the dress she wet playing in the branch. At the age of eleven, extending his chivalry to all womankind, Quentin fights in defense of his teacher when a schoolmate wants to put a frog in her desk (86). At another time, while wearing a cast for a recently broken leg, he "lays for" one of Caddy's callers with a piece of coal (132). Of course, the most important scenes showing his obsession with Caddy's sexual purity are the ones centering around her relationship with Dalton Ames and her marriage to Herbert Head, for as Caddy grows older she gives Quentin real cause to become upset with her violation of traditional forms of behavior.

But why does Quentin settle upon the issue of Caddy's chastity as the initial test by which to judge the possibility of a meaningful life in the present? The answer is found in his response to the tradition. Although he seems to sentimentalize the role of women—and the traditional southern society may itself have done this—certainly he is right in being sensitive to their real importance. As *The Unvanquished* and *Sartoris* show, the matrix of the aristocratic society was the family or clan, and at the center of the clan was the matriarch, the woman, literally holding the group together, "arbitrating from the fireside corner of a crone," as Mr. Compson says in *Absalom, Absalom!*, "the pride and destiny of her family" (69). Cleanth Brooks finds this aspect of Quentin's heritage so crucial that he feels "the themes of woman and fertility are central" in the novel.[6] Brooks is careful not to make Mr. Compson Faulkner's spokesman, but points out that he does express a view of woman "consistently represented in Faulkner's work." The substance of it is that, for Faulkner, "woman is the source and sustainer of virtue, or she is the source of evil. She can be either, because she is, as man is not, always a little beyond good and evil. Faulkner refuses to sentimentalize her . . . [but sees her] as a natural force of tremendous power" (18-19). Faulkner is not, even in filtering the tradition through Quentin's character, suggesting that worship of the woman or the matriarch was the result of woman's central position. The tradition simply had a profound respect for "woman as a natural force of tremendous power."

[6] "Primitivism in *The Sound and the Fury*," in *English Institute Essays, 1952*, ed. Alan S. Downer (New York: Columbia University Press, 1954), p. 26.

The traditional aristocratic society, matriarchal in its organization, was largely Stoic in its rationalization. To the extent that it expressed in its social structure a sexual inequality between men and women, the traditional society was, of course, not Stoic, for in Stoicism this difference is completely absent. The traditional aristocratic society was certainly moral; that is, the system of rules, the positive law, expressed the cumulative experience and wisdom of the historical community's attempt to allow man to function as man. The code held as long as the community participated in and gave automatic assent to the moral vision, the "natural law," of which the code was a rationalization. The Stoic character of the social order is shown in its attitude toward deviation. The man-made moral order did not make a place for personal guilt. Individuality, self-reliance, proper pride, courage, and the like were virtues, but defection with respect to them was simply crime—a mistake, a failure of nerve, a loss of humanity. A "sin" was always an act of social deviation. There was no question of forgiveness since, rationally speaking, there was no reason for deviation.

The forms of honorable behavior for women were creations of rational men, not women. The woman remained sovereign, beyond the rules. *"Women only use other people's codes of honour,"* says Quentin's father (*SF*, 193). Brooks points out that the masculinized Drusilla and Joanna Burden are destroyed by their inflexible allegiance to a rationalized code, while Aunt Jenny Du Pre and Rosa Millard, though "stout holders of family order and honor," remain women, "a little above and outside the codes that their menfolk have to follow" (20). Bayard of *The Unvanquished* says in the late 1860's, "times are never strange to women: . . . it is just one continuous monotonous thing full of the repeated follies of their menfolks" (223). That the woman as woman is not tied to the code is evidenced by Drusilla's and Aunt Jenny's different reactions to Bayard's refusal to shoot his father's killer. At fifteen Bayard hunted down and shot Grumby, the murderer of his grandmother (Rosa Millard), but, when a man, he faced Redmond, his father's killer, unarmed. The revolutionary character of this last act lay in its fulfilling but also transcending the code, and the power of it is dramatized by Redmond's leaving Jefferson never to return. Bayard's act was a heroic witness to another orientation, one in which courage is exhibited not in facing death (though, fulfilling the Stoic code, Bayard did that) but in facing one's own (his family's) guilt. When George Wyatt, a member of Colonel Sartoris' old troop and his devoted friend, catches the vision of Bayard's new courage, it is in a "pale bleak stare which was speculative *yet not at all ratiocinative.* 'Well by God,' he said. '—Do you want a drink?' " (*U,* 288, italics mine).

Bayard's action and the attendant responses by George Wyatt and Aunt Jenny ("So you had a perfectly splendid Saturday afternoon, didn't you? Tell me about it" [292]) point up by contrast the extent of Quentin's truncated feeling for the tradition and lead to some insights into his failure to find final courage. Quentin is moralistic in his attitude rather than moral. He does not participate in the culture in which Bayard stood so deeply that he could transcend it. Paul Tillich, who defines moralism as "the distortion of the moral imperative into an oppressive law," points out that "moral systems, just because of their intimate connection with a cultural system, have the tendency to become oppressive if the general cultural scheme changes. They tend to produce moralism as an attitude."[7] Quentin, who is cut off from the Stoic spirit informing the culture, cannot face the moral problem the codes rationalized, but does appropriate the rationalizations. There is no contradiction in this with his puritan temperament; rather, his puritan legalism is ful-

[7] In *Theology of Culture,* ed. Robert C. Kimball (New York: Oxford University Press, 1959), p. 133.

filled in his focus upon culturally bound forms of justice. Like Judaic law, puritan legalism issues into self-righteousness (Quentin's initial condition) or despair (his final condition) or indifference (Caddy's attitude). When it is not internalized but remains focused upon exterior objects (Caddy loved Quentin, "accepting the fact that he must value above all not her but the virginity of which she was custodian and on which she placed no value whatever" [*SF*, 10]), it becomes, as was Drusilla's kiss to Bayard, an "empty and formal gesture" (*U*, 263), a Pharisaic ritual. In Quentin's last phase, lacking any longer an object for his moralism, he is driven to the abyss of meaninglessness where, also lacking Stoic courage and, blind to personal guilt, refusing grace, he commits suicide.

The tradition testifies that Quentin is rationally right in focusing upon Caddy's frail chastity. His rationalistic and moralistic sensibility allows him to salvage from the tradition only an ability to identify its talismans, its fetishes, and does not afford him a vision beyond the *mise en scène* to the vital spirit generating the code itself. In his mind, his inherited concept of honor (and thus the status of meaning) is more than figuratively supported "by the minute fragile membrane of her maidenhead" (*SF*, 9). It is also true that the decline and fall of the Compson family is paced by the decline and fall of the woman from a position of virtuous eminence. Not only in Caddy but also in his mother does Quentin find no assent to the moral vision of which the code was a rationalization. Brooks is therefore right when he says that the failure of Quentin's mother is just as crucial as Caddy's failure and has a great deal to do with Caddy's incapacity.[8] Herbert Head's bourgeois excuse for his past ("I never had a mother like yours to teach me the finer points" [128]) heightens the poignancy of Quentin's inner cry, *"My little sister had no. If I could say Mother. Mother"* (114), and

8 Brooks, in *English Institute Essays*, pp. 14-15.

again, *"if I'd just had a mother so I could say Mother Mother"* (190). Quentin has no mother; he does not enjoy the matriarchal structure under which the code of honor functions to provide meaning.

Quentin's obsession with sex—and it is that—certainly goes beyond its function in his inherited code. He is sick with his sister's honeysuckle sweet sex, but he is also perversely attracted to it. When Caddy finds him in the barn during the rain with Natalie *"dancing sitting down"* (154, 155), he jumps into the hog wallow, in a highly symbolic action, and smears her with mud. Benjy, of course, is sensitive to Caddy's loss of chastity too, and also relates to her sexually, but his attraction is, in the novel's dramatic context, less perverted, more innocent, less moralistic, more moral and forgiving.

Caddy's failure is not from sheer perversity; she fails in Quentin's terms, not her own. Her experiments in sex are "natural," if foolish. She is capable of compassion and love, as her relationship with Benjy and her love for Dalton Ames illustrate. The pathetic irony of Quentin's situation comes from his incapacity, not hers. She is capable—or was before he corrupted her—of the natural power and fertility of the matriarch. Caddy actually functions as a mother to Benjy. When, during Quentin's second phase, she succumbs to his rationalistic moralism, she divests herself of that sovereignty essential to the matriarch—the sovereignty above the rules. Quentin's agony, arising from his myopic moralism, is heightened by the fact that he has not only a promiscuous sister, but also a sister who will not admit, does not know, and cannot believe that her promiscuity involves anything more than a private and personal doom.

Although only with reference to Caddy can he bring his inherited and present worlds together, Caddy is constitutionally incapable of helping him. Only in the second phase of his private struggle does she begin to share his horror

of sex and admit to being sick in a fairly deep sense: *"There
was something terrible in me sometimes at night I could see
it grinning at me I could see it through them grinning at me"*
(131), and *"But now I know I'm dead I tell you"* (143).
Prior to his moralistic taunting, she is innocent; she really
loves Dalton Ames: "yes I hate him I would die for him
I've already died for him I die for him over and over again"
(170). Initially, she is only disquieted in the presence of
Quentin because she does love in him even that "inflexible
corruptless judge of what he considered the family's honor
and its doom" (10), and pities his incapacity to enjoy sexual
experience: "poor Quentin . . . youve never done that have
you . . . that what I have what I did" (170). In the presence
of Benjy, however, she feels judged by what in his blundering way is a forgiving love.

Caddy's incapacity to accept the role demanded of her if
Quentin is to affirm traditional meaning on traditional terms
causes Quentin to change his strategy. In the second phase,
his father becomes important because he redefines Quentin's
problem from one of ethical behavior to one of metaphysics: "time is your misfortune Father said" (123). Time
is his misfortune in many senses. It is the inevitable dimension of historical reality in which meaning resides, as Dilsey
knows, if it resides anywhere, the *sine qua non* of human
experience. When for Quentin the traditional meaning does
not last through time to the present, then life entails a loss
he cannot sustain, exhibits a metaphysical evil with which he
is not prepared to deal. Time is his misfortune because it
has encompassed the breakup of the spiritual center of the
traditional society supporting the values which Quentin insists must be *the* values.

His father, closer to the spirit of the tradition than
Quentin, can see part of Quentin's problem clearly. Quentin's
relationship with Caddy is a specific instance of a general
situation. It is amoral nature, "natural human folly" (195),

not Caddy, that is hurting Quentin. But his father has given up: "Because no battle is ever won he said. They are not even fought. The field only reveals to man his own folly and despair, and victory is an illusion of philosophers and fools" (95). Man is "an unvarying nil: stalemate of dust and desire" (143), and woman a "delicate equilibrium of periodical filth between two moons balanced" (147).

Time and nature—or simply the nature of things—is his father's diagnosis. Quentin, however, has just met defeat by something much more specific—sex. In this second phase he needs in some way to relate sex to time and nature so that by establishing meaning in them he will prove Caddy's sexual deviations meaningful. He accepts his father's conclusion that his condition is a function of time's misfortune, but is not yet willing to concede that some meaning cannot be saved. If he can outrage time and nature by some act so serious that his father and Caddy cannot deny its seriousness, he will establish, if only negatively, some meaning in the nature of things: "If we could just have done something so dreadful that they would have fled hell except us" (98). Thus it is that incest becomes the means by which he can at once relate himself to Caddy's world of experience, give significance to her world, and isolate himself with her in an eternal atonement for their violation of meaning.

That Quentin settles upon incest indicates how uncanny he can be in his desperation. It involves him in a fundamental shift from a Stoic to a Christian reference. If a sin, incest is a sin of the flesh, an unnatural human sin as opposed to a "natural human folly." By contemplating a deliberate act which is sinful rather than merely criminal, Quentin invokes a Christian moral order—though a greatly attenuated one, it must be said—which crushes man not because of his finitude but because of his guilt. Incest is a sin linked in such a way to his first and unsuccessful strategy that he can save something of traditional meaning even if on nontraditional terms. It is not merely a flaunting of the social code of honor, a violation of society's familial structure; it is a corruption of the heart of a rigid Calvinism which claims to discern a moral order independent of social consent of sinful man. Quentin's uncanny strategy is to coerce damnation in terms which will relate his life to traditional structures of meaning.

It must be said that Quentin cheats. He is so involved in his private problem, so intent upon redeeming a time no longer present, that his second strategy is mostly a struggle within his own mind and is anchored in objective reality only by its requirement that Caddy and his father concur. Caddy must know what is involved; she must lose her natural amorality and accept his restructuring of her world: *"I'll tell Father then itll have to be because you love Father then we'll have to go away amid the pointing and the horror the clean flame I'll make you say we did I'm stronger than you I'll make you know we did you thought it was them but it was me listen I fooled you"* (167). And Mr. Compson must be convinced that Quentin's true relationship with Caddy is incestuous and sinful, since against his father's cynicism his whole desperate strategy has been forged. Quentin cannot trust Caddy with actual incest: "i was afraid to i was afraid she might and then it wouldnt have done any good but if i could tell you we did it would have been so" (195). Quentin cannot, in fact, trust the real world at all. It has forced open his hoard of traditional values and left him gazing upon their destruction.

The second strategy fails because Quentin receives no support from Caddy and his father. Caddy's reply to his threat to tell father is, *"I dont give a goddam what you do"* (157), and his father responds with "people cannot do anything that dreadful they cannot do anything very dreadful at all" (99). This second failure leaves him with one last move, depending upon no one but himself. "You can shirk all things," he responds to his father, as he tells himself,

"It's not when you realise that nothing can help you—religion, pride, anything—it's when you realise that you dont need any aid" (99).

Quentin's report of the events of his last day—including the recollections of past events—should be read in the light of his third phase, his condition at the point of suicide. The precipitant, unsorted, and dreamlike character of his recollections is accounted for by the fact that he has reached the point where the past has completely pre-empted his consciousness. Present occurrences trigger recollections and take on a fixity as he relates them to his past. The complex symbolism of shadow, door, bird, slanting, clocks, honeysuckle, flowers, wistaria, water—in short, all the sounds, feelings, smells, and sights associated with what are in his consciousness the significant events of his life—reveals the content of all three phases. Each of the symbolic images compresses most of the others. In many of the passages of recollection, one image will evoke others or substitute for others. For example, honeysuckle, probably the most important single image, is associated with water or wetness (rain, drizzle, mist) since the smell of honeysuckle hangs heavily in the wet atmosphere of the crucial hog wallow and suicide compact scenes; it therefore also recalls images of sex and death, of shadow, twilight, greyness, of Benjy's bellowing, of Caddy's marriage, and of time and being. It suffuses his very breath of life: "I had to pant to get any air at all out of that thick grey honeysuckle" (170). Quentin's recapitulation of his life in the sensuous language of symbolic imagery serves at once to render the quality of his sensibility and to reveal the thematic contribution of his section to the novel as a whole.

An analysis of the symbolic imagery shows that Quentin's concern with the loss of meaning is extended to include his personal past. He despairs of preserving in time even the immediacy of his own sensitivity to the loss of meaning and in a last psychotic wrench of his intellect sees life's meaninglessness and emptiness solved by a negation of being itself. At the point of suicide he has completely subjected public reality to his private hurt.

External reality in the final stage is oblique, shaded, and mirrored, not directly and immediately experienced. Its obliquity is indicated from the first moment of his waking as the window sash, catching the light of the morning sun, casts a shadow upon the curtains. A sparrow slants across the sunlight and listens with Quentin to the chimes striking the hour. A bird, or something flying, accompanies him in his recollections as well as in his walk. The hands of the clocks in the jeweler's window are "at a faint angle, like a gull tilting into the wind" (104). The gull image is associated with time (and death) by Quentin's father: "time is your misfortune Father said. A gull on an invisible wire attached through space dragged" (123). The gull becomes the symbol for eternity, the meeting of time and space, as he watches Gerald Bland rowing on the river.

Quentin notices mayflies slanting (136), girls gushing like "swallows swooping" (125), the river glinting "beyond things in sort of swooping glints" (130), and butterflies slanting along in the shade avoiding the slanting sunlight as they play about the boys going for a swim (141). As he tries to talk with the little Italian girl, "little sister," who follows him about silently, he hears "a bird somewhere in the woods, beyond the broken and infrequent slanting of sunlight" whose whistle to him is "a sound meaningless and profound" (154) because he recollects another time—after his empty and hopeless formal gesture of hitting Ames (while standing on the bridge over the water symbolizing Caddy's sexual sin and his own death impulse)—when "the sun slanted and a bird [was] singing somewhere beyond the sun" (179).

At that time, too, Ames appeared as if Quentin were "looking at him through a piece of coloured glass" (180), and as Quentin sought the shade of a tree, still stunned from fainting (Ames had not hit him), he "heard the bird again and the water and then everything sort of rolled away and I didnt feel anything at all I felt almost good after all those days and the nights with honeysuckle coming up out of the darkness into my room where I was trying to sleep" (180-81). And finally, Caddy's eyes, which were like cornered rats when Benjy smelled her sin with Dalton Ames (168), become empty "like the eyes in the statues blank and unseeing and serene" (182) as she repeats Ames's name and looks "off into the trees where the sun slanted and where the bird [sang]" (182). Immediately after this recollection Quentin feels his own eye "dead" and tries to see himself—by reflection—in the water in which Shreve is bathing it, since, as he learns, he has just had a fight with Bland.

The feel of obliquity is reinforced by Quentin's awareness of ascent and descent. Benjy reports that after Caddy had splashed Quentin with water in the branch scene, Quentin watched the others go up the hill toward the lights of the house (42). Years later, Quentin runs back down the hill toward the branch and out of Benjy's bellowing where he finds Caddy lying half in the branch, "the water flowing about her hips" (168). Then, after a fumbling suicide attempt, with overtones of incest, they ascend the hill again (172) to meet Dalton Ames, where again, Caddy's and Ames's shadows merge in an image of obliquity to form one shadow with her head above his (173), and then the reverse, Ames's shadow high with Caddy's face becoming blurred (174), appearing to Quentin as *"the beast with two backs"* (167).

Quentin is particularly sensitive to shadow since he identifies his own coming death with shadow. He seems attracted to the Negro lore that "a drowned man's shadow was watching for him in the water all the time" (109), and several times feels he has "tricked" (109, 111, 114, 153) his shadow out of the water to follow him and allow him to tramp upon it (the shadow is an image of the body which he shall soon do away with): "trampling my shadow's bones into the concrete" (115), "walked upon the belly of my shadow" (115), "treading my shadow into pavement" (119), and "I stood in the belly of my shadow" (119). The "trick" is in accord with his whole personal attack upon reality, his refusal to recognize reality's inexorable warning when the shadow of the sash on the curtains put him "in time again, hearing the watch" (95). Even his own death as shadow is not, as his father recognizes, truly real to him: "you seem to regard it merely as an experience that will whiten your hair overnight so to speak without altering your appearance at all" (196). Shadow, shade, darkness, greyness, twilight are also somewhat equivalent to all sex. It was in the twilight that he first met Dalton Ames with Caddy, but his own virginity and self-identity are threatened by "so many of them walking along in the shadows and whispering with their soft girlvoices lingering in the shadowy places and the words coming out and perfume and eyes you could feel not see, but if it was that simple to do it wouldnt be anything *and if it wasnt anything, what was I*" (166, italics mine). Mrs. Bland, breaking into his reverie, appropriately diagnoses his case with the question, "Quentin? Is he sick, Mr MacKenzie?" (166).

The obliquity of external reality to Quentin is apparent in its slanted, shaded, half-hidden and mysterious character and also in its appearance as reflected and not directly present. To find himself after his fight with Bland, Quentin looks for his reflection in the water basin (182). He gazes over the side of a bridge spanning the Charles River, looking for his shadow, narcissistically seeking the profile of his death there, tricking it out of the water (it is, after all, a reflection of his body and not of his intellectual being) to refrain a while longer "from the waiting willing friendly tender incredible body of his beloved" (9). His entire last day is a courtship of death; Julio's charge has symbolic substance; "You steala my seester" (158). Quentin's thievery (his namesake was also a thief) was of Caddy's innocence and now it is of his own life. Caddy found death *for him* at French Lick. His recollection of Caddy's marriage (only thirty-eight days before the time of his narration) is mirrored, shadowed, substanceless, and dominated by Benjy's bellowing:

> *Only she was running already when I heard it* [Benjy's bellowing]. *In the mirror she was running before I knew what it was. That quick, her train caught up over her arm she ran out of the mirror like a cloud, her veil swirling in long glints her heels brittle and fast clutching her dress onto her shoulder with the other hand, running out of the mirror the smells roses roses the voice that breathed o'er Eden. Then she was across the porch I couldn't hear her heels then in the moonlight like a cloud, the floating shadow of the veil running across the grass, into the bellowing.* (100-01)

In the last paragraph of his section, Quentin symbolically measures external reality again in the mirror. He looks for the bloodstain on his vest: "in the mirror the stain didnt show. Not like my eye did, anyway" (197).

The images of obliquity, then, pile up, come pell-mell—slanting, shadow, reflection—as Quentin reports and recalls. His final condition shows him to have fixed his life in images which allow reality to present experience only in their terms. The images reveal his final condition as one in which he despairs of sustaining the meaning he has demanded of life; they show him estranged from any reference wider than his private problem, symbolically forcing the question of ultimate meaning, and finding experience to yield only emptiness. Faulkner affords Quentin a sentence near the end of his section which summarizes, in some of the familiar symbolic images, the three stages of his problem. Through his mind runs the question, when will the smell of wistaria stop?

> Sometimes I could put myself to sleep saying that over and over
> until after the honeysuckle got all mixed up in it the whole
> thing came to symbolise night and unrest I seemed to be lying
> neither asleep nor awake looking down a long corridor of grey
> halflight where *all stable things had become shadowy paradoxical*
> all I had done shadows all I had felt suffered taking visible form
> antic and perverse mocking without relevance inherent themselves
> with the denial of the significance they should have affirmed
> thinking *I was I was not who was not was not who.* (188,
> italics mine)

In this passage, the smell of wistaria is associated with his
mother's sickness, her incapacity to function as a mother.
This odor yields to honeysuckle as he fixes upon Caddy as
the sex object embodying his problem of meaning. Then
night, unrest, a long corridor of grey half-light, and shadow
dominate his consciousness as his problem is stated in the
abstract terms of time and being.

Immediately following this reverie Quentin reports that
he "could smell the curves of the river beyond the dusk" and
could see "the last light supine and tranquil upon tideflats
like pieces of broken mirror" (188). Reality is fractured
in Quentin's broken mirror, but in "the river beyond the
dusk" he will seek in drowning his "refuge unfailing[,] in
which conflict [is] tempered[,] silenced [and] reconciled"
(188-89). He sees his suicide as a seeking of silence. Moving
from sex through time to pose the problem of being itself,
he despairs of saving meaning. He seeks the silence of non-
being in the swift and peaceful water of the river, where he
can, as he could not with Caddy, isolate himself "out of the
loud world" and let the world "roar away" (195)—its ticking watches, clanging chimes, and the bellowing and moan-
ing of Benjy. His father expresses for him the object of this
last desperate strategy: "you are contemplating an apotheosis
in which a temporary state of mind will become symmetrical

above the flesh and aware both of itself and of the flesh it will not quite discard you will not even be dead" (195-96). Quentin affirms his father's statement by the single word "temporary." His father then touches the heart of the matter: "you cannot bear to think that someday it will no longer hurt you like this" (196).

Quentin's suicide, then, arises from despair at the prospect of time's dulling even the meager meaning he has salvaged— his own hurt. He is anxious about ultimate meaninglessness and emptiness in time. His is a peculiarly modern as opposed to a Stoic or Christian anxiety. Anxiety of meaninglessness is, in Tillich's terms, "anxiety about the loss of an ultimate concern, of a meaning which gives meaning to all meanings." Tillich goes on to describe Quentin's situation almost exactly when he spells out the source of the anxieties of meaninglessness and emptiness:

> This anxiety [of meaninglessness] is aroused by the loss of a spiritual center, of an answer, however symbolic and indirect, to the question of the meaning of existence.
>
> The anxiety of emptiness is aroused by the threat of nonbeing to the special contents of the spiritual life. A belief breaks down through external events or inner processes: one is cut off from creative participation in a sphere of culture, one feels frustrated about something which one had passionately affirmed. . . . Everything is tried and nothing satisfies. The contents of the tradition, however excellent, however praised, however loved once, lose their power to give content *today*.[9]

V

The theme of the negative status of meaning finds a second rendering in the novel's other major action, spanning the years 1910-1928, involving the conflict between

---

[9] *The Courage to Be*, pp. 47-48.

Jason and Miss Quentin and reaching its climax in the theft
of Jason's hoard. The reader comes to Jason's section, too,
having before him Benjy's faithful reports of events from
the entire period, up through the day of Miss Quentin's theft.
Jason's narration, focusing on the day prior to the theft, is,
like Quentin's, of events already in the past so far as the
reader is concerned. What Jason has to say comes to the
reader from a perspective which, though short, is sufficient
to give hint of the impending denouement and thus to
heighten the intrinsically ironical effect of his report. Here
again, Faulkner's apparently arbitrary scrambling of chronology has a literary function. But the fullest development
of the second action begins in the conscious reverie of Jason's
section and is completed in the omniscient narrative of
Section IV.

Although the dominant theme remains the same in Jason's
section, an abrupt shift occurs in both the character of the
narrator and the narrative technique. Together these two
accomplish a shift of emphasis within the theme from the
loss of meaning to the complete absence of meaning. Quentin's matter-of-fact ending, "I had forgotten to brush it too,
but Shreve had a brush, so I didnt have to open the bag any
more" (197), is almost serenely sane in contrast to the
emotionally charged, condensed subconscious monologue
preceding it. Jason's opening pseudo aphorism, "Once a
bitch always a bitch, what I say" (198), shows Faulkner
has abandoned high seriousness for comic irony. Quentin,
suffering from loss of meaning as the tradition had defined
it and incapable of finding a new and vital meaning to re-
place it, ultimately destroys himself. Jason does not have
that problem. For him, the tradition is important only to
the degree it gives him social status (256). Meaning lies
somewhere else, in the gaining of his own practical ends,
and he would destroy whatever would frustrate the achievement of those ends—Benjy, Dilsey, Caddy, and Miss Quen-

tin, certainly, but also Lorraine and Mrs. Compson as well as the pigeons and sparrows in the courthouse yard and the stock and dogs which might eat the poison meant for them.

The development of theme in Jason's section is subtly tied to his character. Superficially, it would appear that the status of meaning is not at issue. As with Benjy and Quentin, the events upon which he focuses are those most dear to his own sense of meaning, but the interpretative schemes or ideas he is able to bring to those experiences are vastly attenuated by his self-seeking. Quentin was, of course, concerned with himself, but the meaning he felt to be at stake was a general one, informing all of life. Benjy, since he is an idiot, does not easily qualify for a contrast with Jason in this regard, yet one can see that his moments of greatest feeling are of outgoing love, however ineffectual and pathetic his concern for others might finally be. With Jason, whatever meaning is present is purely personal and is given credence only insofar as it has pragmatic value for achieving goals which are themselves never examined for intrinsic value.

As Jason runs through the events of his day, telling of his various encounters—with Job, the telegraph office, Earl, farmers, drummers—as he recalls and comments upon the history of his relationship with Caddy, her daughter Quentin, with the Negroes of the Compson household, with his mother and Uncle Maury—in short, as he displays the nature and range of his perceptions and interests—two images of him emerge. The first, his self-image, is of one victimized by life, yet able, by virtue of his own righteous strength and consummate rational power, to survive in a world from which he can force the satisfactions of his own rectitude. He was the victim of his father, whose favoritism gave what little was left of the family fortune to Quentin's education and Caddy's wedding. Of his brothers and sisters, "one of them is crazy and another one drowned himself and the other one was turned out into the street by her husband"

(250). Saddled now with a sick and whining mother, responsible for "a kitchen full of niggers to feed" (247), guilty of
"robbing the state asylum of its star freshman" (247), without authority to control his niece whose afternoons are
spent "slipping up and down back alleys" (206-07) with
"town jellybeans" and out-of-town drummers and thereby
compromising his good name, and even duped by New York
Jews on the stock exchange ("I'm not talking about men of
the jewish religion. . . . I have nothing against jews as an
individual. . . . It's just the race" [209]), Jason nevertheless
thinks he has gained a "position in this town" (207), is able
to "stand on . . . [his] own feet" (224), and is "man enough
to keep that flour barrel full" (225). Jason's share in the
Caddy–Herbert Head investment, the bank job in Indiana
which never materialized, is for him the symbol of his total
victimization. It justifies all of his acts of revenge, the
cruelty to Miss Quentin—for him the surrogate symbol for
the job ("Well, they brought my job home tonight" [216])
—and his systematic, long-term theft of the money Caddy
sends for the support of her child.

His self-image is not just a straw man; obviously the very
condition of his life is outrageous. In terms of his own inner
logic, he has indeed been dealt with poorly, and his survival
in the face of his inherited circumstance shows a certain
neurotic vitality. His father *was* an alcoholic, his older
brother a suicide; his sister *is* a prostitute, his brother an
idiot, his niece a bitch, his uncle a toady and a drunkard. He
is a victim of the stock market. Even from without his point
of view, many of the conditions of his life are unjust. This
fact, coupled with the further fact that he is also flatly vicious,
malicious, and without heart or redeeming virtue of any
kind, unless it is his sardonic sense of humor, accounts for
the curious delight the reader finds in his narration.

Perhaps because of his persecution complex he is able to
see through the chicanery and falsity of others. Certainly

the reader is delighted with his insights into Uncle Maury
and his mother: "Little they cared how wet I got, because
then Mother could have a whale of a time being afraid I
was taking pneumonia" (219). Even Dilsey is not totally
immune. When she claims the prerogative of Miss Quentin's
upbringing ("Who else gwine raise her 'cep me? Aint I
raised eve'y one of y'all?"), there is some merit in Jason's
retort, "And a damn fine job you made of it" (216). Some
sympathy for Jason, tending to legitimate the delight found
in his caustic penetration of others, is evoked not only by
the physical suffering of his headaches, whether or not psy-
chosomatic, but also by the thinly veiled torment of his
anxiety over threats to his self-image. At points of stress he
imagines conversations which lay claim to the reader's pity
for his outrageous victimization (260). Throughout, "like I
say," "what I say," and "I always say" drop steadily into the
monologue to buttress his tenuous self-confidence.

But the second image of Jason, the reader's, is quite different. The earlier sections of the novel provide a fairly consistent and transparent symbolic presentation of him as innately selfish and malicious. His hands are often in his
pockets: " 'Jason going to be rich man,' Versh said. 'He
holding his money all the time' " (55, see also 31, 40, 43,
120). Jason plays alone (38), informs on Caddy and Quentin
(43, 93), is fat (43), and overeats; at the time of Damuddy's
death, Quentin stops eating when the children hear their
mother moan, but Jason continues to eat (45); in an early
business enterprise of making and selling kites with the
Patterson boy, Jason is treasurer (113), just as Lycurgus of
ancient Athens was treasurer; and, finally, Caddy fights with
Jason because he cut up some of Benjy's paper dolls (83-84).
These incidents from his early childhood presage the course
and character of his later life.

The second image is confirmed by the dramatic irony of
Jason's narration, an irony, that is, of which Jason, blinded

by his paranoia, is unaware, and it is expanded by the omniscient narrator's comments in the last section. There is for Jason no inconsistency in his generalizations about others—about Jews, Negroes, women, farmers. His treatment of Miss Quentin and Caddy is not cruel; rather, it fulfills the logic of retributive justice, and there is no injustice in his refusal to give Luster a ticket to the carnival. The New York broker, when he fails Jason, is a "damn eastern jew" (209); when he helps him, "an adviser," a "manipulator" (210). Quentin is "a little slut of a girl" (260); Lorraine, "a good honest whore" (251). As a victim of the cotton market, the farmer gets only "a red neck and a hump in his back" (209), but when Earl asks where they would be if it weren't for the farmer, Jason replies, "I'd be home right now . . . Lying down, with an ice pack on my head" (266).

The second image of Jason in its broadest outline is of a man who successfully distorts reality to provide it with a meaning commensurate with his own demands. The world in which he moves exhibits a coherence, an inner logic; it is self-consistent. Jason shares with Quentin a tendency to see meaning as essentially formal, Quentin as he grasps the form of the tradition but misses its spirit, Jason as he depends upon the legal structure of society to protect him in his thievery and to punish his enemies.

In the Appendix, Faulkner says that Jason is "the first sane Compson since before Culloden. . . . Logical rational contained and even a philosopher in the old stoic tradition" (16). Like the Stoic, Jason inlays reality with a patterned meaning which is there so long as he gives it his assent. He appropriates the rational character of the Stoic attitude at those points where he can turn it to use, but he greatly attenuates its humanistic spirit to apply it only to himself. Hence his contractual, legalistic arrangements—with Earl in the hardware business, with Lorraine, whom he schedules for weekends and occasional trips to Memphis, with Caddy,

fulfilling the exact letter of his agreement to show her the
baby Quentin, and even with Dilsey, whose knowledge of
his blackmail provides for her a place in the household until
Caroline Compson's death. Like the mythical Jason of
Euripides, boasting to Medea of his magnanimity in bringing her from barbaric Colchis to civilized Greece, incapable
of gratitude and thinking of his ambition only, Jason Compson measures justice exclusively in terms of self-advantage.
For those who do not affect his personal gain, he is willing
to concede some freedom: of Job's slowness, "Well, it's
Earl's business" (268); of Uncle Maury's new financial
scheme, " 'It's your money,' I says. 'If you want to throw it
to the birds even, it's your business' " (242); of the money
the carnival would take out of town, "it was no skin off my
back" (263); and following the first unsuccessful chase after
Miss Quentin, he can rationalize that "it's no business of
mine. If it was my own daughter now it would be different"
(263).

The logic of Jason's "sanity" is reflected in his consistent
reckoning of justice in materialistic terms. Caddy had promised but failed to deliver his job; thus, Miss Quentin is the
legitimate object upon which at once to vent his fury and
from whom to gain recompense. Caddy's failure to send a
check through on the first day of the month—it was six days
late!—*forces* him to lie to his mother (228); Caddy's typical
inconsiderateness in coming to Jefferson once or twice a year,
her failure to carry through on the letter of the contract
Jason made with her to leave town after she had seen the
baby Quentin for "just a minute," is conclusive: regarding
women, "you cant trust a one of them" (228). His public
justification for his various antics and demands is that he
has to hold the family together, whereas actually he tries in
every way to destroy it, to send Benjy to the asylum in
Jackson, to drive Miss Quentin and Dilsey away. At a more
symbolic level he wants to cut off the Compson line com-

pletely with the surgeon's knife, just as he cut Benjy's paper
dolls. Benjy is gelded and Jason recommends the same treatment for Caddy and Miss Quentin. "Well, like I say they
never started soon enough with their cutting, and they quit
too quick. I know at least two more that needed something
like that, and one of them not over a mile away, either"
(280).

There is in his sane world no question of guilt or innocence
in a Christian sense, but only of criminal defection from the
attenuated norm, a norm established with reference to his
cash advantage. "I'm glad I haven't got the sort of conscience I've got to nurse like a sick puppy all the time"
(246). It is legitimate to claim that Benjy should be sent
to the state asylum to "get that much benefit out of the
taxes we pay" (239), and that the land sold to send Quentin
to Harvard wasted the tax paid to support the state university (250). Parson Walthall pays no taxes and therefore has
no right to protect the pigeons in the courthouse yard. It is
impossible for Jason to suspend in even the most minor instance the standard of cash reckoning which is built into a
just (sane) order of things. He cannot give the show ticket
to Luster; he must sell it or burn it.

To say that Jason is "the first sane Compson since before
Culloden" is to point up that Jason is not really a Compson
at all. "All the Compson gave out before it got to me"
(215), he believes, and his mother's refrain is just as
accurate: he is "not a Compson except in name" (214). In
Jason there is nothing of "that long line of men who had
had something in them of decency and pride" (13); we are
told that he "ends" such a line. Jason survives because he
successfully "fended off and held his own *with Compsons*"
(16, my italics). To Caddy but also to the reader he proves
himself "a different breed of cat from Father" (219).

To what great extent Jason depends upon the structure
of justice in society to be rational in accord with his private

norm of rationality is epitomized by his reaction to its failure
to protect him from the blow of Miss Quentin's capricious
robbery. He tells the sheriff, "That's my business where I
keep my money. Your business is to help me get it back"
(319). Convinced more than ever of the injustice of his injury, and even "seeming to get an actual pleasure out of his
outrage and impotence" (319), he imagines, after the
sheriff's refusal to help him, scenes in which his righteous
will triumphs over the very forces of circumstance and destiny: " 'And damn You, too,' he said [to Circumstance],
'See if You can stop me,' thinking of himself, his file of
soldiers with the manacled sheriff in the rear, dragging
Omnipotence down from His throne, if necessary; of the
embattled legions of both hell and heaven through which
he tore his way and put his hands at last on his fleeing niece"
(322). Even more devastating than the loss of the money itself is his having been "outwitted by a woman, a girl. . . .
by the very symbol of the lost job itself, and worst of all,
by a bitch of a girl" (323). When he visualizes himself
recomposing the shattered structure of his world by "entering the courthouse with a file of soldiers and dragging the
sheriff out," it is of the job, not the money or his niece, he
thinks: "Thinks he can sit with his hands folded and see me
lose my job. I'll show him about jobs" (321). The job, of
course, had been lost eighteen years earlier.

The point is that although his sane world is strained, it
does not collapse. He founders on the wreck of his own
rational scheme, but never admits its essential fallaciousness.
His reaction to the public spectacle Benjy makes in the last
scene of the novel and his subsequent history as given in the
Appendix and in *The Mansion* show that he survives his
defeat without learning anything of importance from it.
The fact is, if he is to remain "sane," Jason cannot afford to
learn from his defeat, for the only lesson it could teach
him would be one which would undermine his already

tenuous world of meaning and discover him incapable of accepting a world in which guilt and sin rather than simple criminal defection from a privately rationalized code describe causality of events. Such a world would be "opposed to all nature and contrary to the whole rhythm of events" (324).

Consequently, Jason's sanity—"logical rational contained" —is what damns him. In itself and in its relationship to other characters in the novel, his sanity is the horror of him. As his character begins to become clear in the dramatic irony of his self-revelation and in his reaction to the events of Easter Sunday, the second side of the novel's first major theme emerges with force: if his world, void of a meaning adequate for a true affirmation of experience, is the only world possible for a meaningful life, then life's sound and fury signify nothing.

In the novel itself, it is the old Negro Job who expresses the final judgment on Jason. Job can deal with Jason, beating him in an exchange of words, because he has nothing at stake to defend before Jason. "I works to suit de man whut pays me Sat'dy night" (207), Job tells him. " 'I wont try to fool you,' he says. 'You too smart fer me' " (267). Lacking Jason's self-importance, he also lacks his insecurity. His sympathy with the boll weevil, though prosaic, is genuine, for to him all of the simple human pleasures do not come by hot pursuit: "Boll-weevil got tough time. Work ev'y day in de week out in de hot sun, rain er shine. Aint got no front porch to set on en watch de wattermilyuns growin and Sat'dy dont mean nothin a-tall to him" (208). Jason, doing his work for the day in the hot sun—pursuing Miss Quentin and the man in the red tie—finds nature hostile, vigorously engaged in a personal attack upon him:

> the sun getting down just to where it could shine straight into my eyes. . . . beggar lice and twigs and stuff all over me, inside my clothes and shoes and all, . . . my hand right on a bunch of poison oak. . . . With the sun and all in my eyes and my blood

going so I kept thinking every time my head would go on and
burst and get it over with, with briers and things *grabbing at me*.
(258-59, italics mine)

Job's simple honesty about his own limitations and his unwillingness to accept Jason's criteria of meaning give him a
wisdom alien to Jason's narrow world:

"Aint a man in dis town kin keep up wid you fer smartness.
You fools a man whut so smart he cant even keep up wid hisself," he says, getting in the wagon and unwrapping the reins.
    "Who's that?" I says.
    "Dat's Mr Jason Compson," he says. "Git up dar, Dan!" (267)

Jason's section closes on the same note on which it opened:
"Once a bitch always a bitch, what I say." The last paragraph rehearses in order all the sources of his misery and
invokes the full spread of his claims for pity:

I could hear the Great American Gelding snoring away like a
planing mill. . . . And if they'd just sent him on to Jackson
while he was under the ether, he'd never have known the difference [Benjy]. But that would have been too simple for a
Compson to think of [the Compsons]. . . . Well, like I say they
never started soon enough with their cutting, and they quit too
quick. I know at least two more that needed something like that,
and one of them not over a mile away, either. . . . Like I say
once a bitch always a bitch [Caddy and Miss Quentin]. . . .
I dont want to make a killing; save that to suck in the smart
gamblers with. I just want an even chance to get my money back
[the New York Jews]. And once I've done that they can bring
all Beale Street and all bedlam in here and two of them can sleep
in my bed and another one can have my place at the table too
[Negroes]. (280)

Faulkner has said of Jason that he represents "complete
evil" (*FN*, 104). Yet we have seen that he is more complex
than that. Indeed, in many ways Jason is the most complex
character of the novel, and the most difficult to assess. In

a sense, Faulkner did not finish with a final judgment of
him or even with a final characterization. It took at least
three more novels, the Snopes trilogy, to characterize those
elements which distinguish Jason from the Compson-
Sartoris-McCaslin tradition. This is not to say that Jason is
merely a Snopes. His defeat by Flem Snopes in *The Mansion*
comes about because Flem is able to depend upon a false aristocratic pride in Jason, who envisages the Jefferson airport
as "Compson Field." It should be noted, also, that when
Faulkner expanded the later Compson history in the Appendix, Jason was given more space by far than any other
Compson.

In the novel itself, Jason is not a character of complete
evil. Faulkner's art is better than his literary criticism. Jason
is demonic rather than satanic. A character of complete evil
could not convince, delight, or even horrify as does Jason.
His complexity in the novel is most easily understood, I
believe, if we set it forth in the terms of "irony" and "pathos"
as Reinhold Niebuhr has so carefully defined them in another context. In the Preface to *The Irony of American History,* Niebuhr says:

> Pathos is that element in an historic situation which elicits pity,
> but neither deserves admiration nor warrants contrition. Pathos
> arises from fortuitous cross-purposes and confusions in life for
> which no reason can be given, or guilt ascribed. Suffering caused
> by purely natural evil is the clearest instance of the purely
> pathetic. . . . Irony consists of apparently fortuitous incongruities
> in life which are discovered, upon closer examination, to be not
> merely fortuitous. Incongruity as such is merely comic. It elicits
> laughter. This element of comedy is never completely eliminated
> from irony. But irony is something more than comedy. A comic
> situation is proved to be an ironic one if a hidden relation is
> discovered in the incongruity. If virtue becomes vice through
> some hidden defect in the virtue; if strength becomes weakness
> because of the vanity to which strength may prompt the mighty
> man or nation; if security is transmuted into insecurity because

too much reliance is placed upon it; if wisdom becomes folly because it does not know its own limits—in all such cases the situation is ironic. The ironic situation is distinguished from a pathetic one by the fact that the person involved in it bears some responsibility for it. . . . While a pathetic . . . situation is not dissolved when a person becomes conscious of his involvement in it, an ironic situation must dissolve, if men or nations are made aware of their complicity in it. Such awareness involves some realization of the hidden vanity or pretension by which comedy is turned into irony. This realization either must lead to an abatement of the pretension, which means contrition; or it leads to a desperate accentuation of the vanities to the point where irony turns into pure evil.[10]

Now, we have seen that the thematic development through Jason's character depends upon irony in two ways. There is first of all the irony Jason employs in his dealings with others. Some of this has elements of real comedy. His remarks about Job, who was uncrating the cultivators "at the rate of about three bolts to the hour" (207), or about the Negro who brought him his car "after about a week" (235), are characteristic of frontier humor, a humor still found in the comic exaggeration of J. D. Salinger's city hero, Holden Caulfield. Jason's humor, like Holden's, is a camouflage for an acute anxiety, in Jason's case an anxiety about the profit lost with the loss of time. Jason's contrived account at the dinner table of his having loaned his car to a showman to chase "his sister's husband [who] was out riding with some town woman" (275), however, shows irony becoming simple cruelty. He also becomes cruel at the points where he finds himself really threatened: unequal to the objective distance irony requires, he engages in direct, sardonic attack.

On this first level of irony we can also put Jason's situ-

---

[10] *The Irony of American History* (New York: Charles Scribner's Sons, 1952), pp. vii-viii.

ation. The historical situation of the Compsons seems pregnant with an evil not of Jason's making: he is heir to
"apparently fortuitous incongruities in life." Closer exami-
nation shows that the incongruities in his heritage are not
merely fortuitous but that the tradition is morally deficient
at a crucial point and that the natural (inherited) evil of
the present situation is the result, in large measure, of a
moral failure hidden in the southern (Compson) past. Just
what the nature and extent of this moral failure is, is examined in the two other Yoknapatawpha stories with which
we deal, *Absalom, Absalom!,* accounting for it in Stoic but
chiefly Christian terms, and "The Bear," which yields an
orthodox Christian interpretation. In *The Sound and the
Fury,* the Stoic and Christian judgments are counterpoised
and fused somewhat ambiguously.

Further, the evil of Jason's situation is only apparently
fortuitous to the extent that he is partly responsible for it.
Jason is dimly aware that many of the things he does are
wrong, but he is able to rationalize them successfully. He
tells his story to the sheriff with "his sense of injury and
impotence feeding upon its own sound" (318). The very
energy with which he attacks others who threaten him, the
pitch of his anxiety showing through at moments of rationalization, the circuitous movements through which he must
go to deceive others (to counterfeit checks, for example),
the plaintiveness of his appeals to sympathy—these are evidences of his awareness of responsibility. His complicity
does not, however, take the route of contrition but the route
of "desperate accentuation of the vanities to the point where
irony turns into pure evil."

We find, then, in both instances of the first use of irony,
that the ironic situation tends to evolve into the pathetic.
In the first instance, Jason's own use of irony is not sustained.
When he is threatened, he begins to hurt, deeply to hurt,
others. The comedy of the narration is shattered by the

pathos of Caddy's hysterical laughter in the face of Jason's cruelty, for example, or by her and her daughter's identical cries of despair, sounded sixteen years apart—"Oh God, oh God" (227, 233). In the second instance, we find that Jason's situation is pathetic insofar as he suffers from an inherited evil and that the pathos is compounded to the extent he refuses to admit his complicity. His situation therefore elicits pity, but in no way can he be admired. He makes no attempt at amelioration, involves himself in no general attack upon the situation as such. In fact, he uses, manipulates, the situation to his own advantage; turns the evil into a cash asset, capitalizing on Caddy's plight, Miss Quentin's defenselessness, and his mother's self-pity. In his suggestion that Benjy be rented to a sideshow, no genuine good humor is involved. Jason would do just that were it possible without hurting his reputation. And, of course, that he should joke about it in commercial terms is characteristic.

The second level of irony is dramatic, obtaining only between the reader and the document. Jason has much truth to tell of the Compsons, especially of himself as he shows how well he can deceive himself. This irony also contains some elements of the comic. There is comic incongruity in his gross inconsistencies which arise from and find their justification in the unrelieved logical and emotional consistency of his self-centeredness. His monologue becomes, at this level, the self-damning revelation of a crass opportunist. But again, the ironic element gives way to the pathetic. As he misinterprets the events of his life to indicate his own strength, wisdom, and virtue, a price of real suffering is paid by others; to them—to Caddy, Miss Quentin, Dilsey, Luster —Jason's activity has the force of an evil over which they have only slight control. Because of their situation they thus elicit pity, but they are not to be admired simply for the reason of their suffering.

Besides the two uses of irony already distinguished, there

is another, the ironic stance of Faulkner himself as he works behind and through the novel to juxtapose, to intensify but not to resolve the thematic conflicts. An important aspect of this third irony is in the events of the novel. Benjy is initially named after Uncle Maury; Quentin tries to find a mother for "little sister"; Benjy confuses in his memory a funeral with a wedding; Benjy imposes his order upon Jason as he rides past the Confederate monument; and Jason is frustrated by the very forces of law by which he was able to steal money from Miss Quentin when she, without premeditation, undoes in one irrational act all that he had so rationally executed. Such events—and there are others—suggest a moral order of some kind, an order, Christian in many aspects, of retribution and compensation.

But one is aware of an even more terrible irony at work, an irony bordering on skepticism. For as Jason desperately accentuates his vanities to the point of pure evil, he appears in many respects innately incapable of any other response. If for the moment we can think of Dilsey as exemplifying the appropriate and saving response to the situation of the Compsons in 1928, we see in contrast that Jason seems temperamentally, psychologically, and even biologically so constituted that he *cannot* respond with love or forgiveness or even a natural human kindness to others. To the extent that there is this note of skeptical despair in Faulkner, it roots in the Stoic side of his estimate of man. Fate has dealt unevenly with men. Not all men in the Stoic scheme are capable of the response of the wise man; indeed, the mass of men are blatantly common. Jason simply does not as a human being have what it takes. To this extent, his character exhibits a natural evil, not a distinctly human one, which in turn causes real suffering. In the fact that Faulkner does not in the novel's final issue allow this note to emerge as purely skeptical, we can see something of a Calvinistic judgment on his part upon the predamned.

Cleanth Brooks has said that Thomas Sutpen of *Absalom,*

Absalom! is "innocent" in the sense that he never grows, never learns about the nature of reality.[11] This germinative thought is carried over by Lawrence E. Bowling to apply to all of the Compson children. Jason, however, is "both guilty and innocent. He is guilty in the sense that he wilfully commits innumerable actions which he knows to be immoral and vicious; but he is innocent in the sense that he remains ignorant of basic human principles."[12] "Guilt" and "innocence," as the terms are used by Brooks and Bowling, help illuminate Jason's character. Jason never "knows"; he remains innocent in much the same way Caddy was innocent before her capitulation to Quentin's judgment. But the mere fact of Jason's ungrowing, unlearning presence in the novel where Dilsey and Benjy have basically different reactions to the same events is evidence of a tension within Faulkner's total view of man. It can be seen as a tension between a Christian humanism which refuses to solve the paradox of good and evil in a Manichaean manner and a Stoicism which simply shakes its angry fist at the universe. Or it can be seen as a tension between a Christian view of man's tragic dilemma on the one hand, in which evil (the traditional, inherited evil from a morally deficient southern past), though destructive, can be the occasion for a new, emergent goodness, and, on the other hand, a metaphysics of pathos such as Mr. Compson's which can see no sin but only "natural human folly."

VI

The second major theme of *The Sound and the Fury*, the positive status of meaning in experience, is achieved

11 "*Absalom, Absalom:* The Definition of Innocence," *The Sewanee Review*, LXI (Autumn 1951), 545.

12 Bowling, "Faulkner and the Theme of Innocence," *The Kenyon Review*, 475.

by refraction of the two main actions through the characters
of Benjy and Dilsey. The Quentin–Caddy–Mr. Compson
action, embodying meaning's loss, appears in Benjy's experience to sustain meaning's presence, while the Jason–Miss
Quentin action as experienced by Dilsey testifies to meaning's endurance as opposed to its absence. Both Benjy and
Dilsey stand in something of a choric relationship to the
two main actions, reflecting, responding to, interpreting
(dramatically, not intellectually) the events of the novel.
Dilsey, however, also involves herself directly in the action.

The depth and richness of the meaning to which Benjy
is witness is difficult to measure, but its intensity is apparent,
even if his response to it is not efficacious. The chief temp-
tation in presenting Benjy as an agent of the novel's positive
theme is to claim too much for him, to forget that he is an
idiot and that the irrationality of his response is no answer
to the faulty rationality of either Quentin or Jason. Chiefly
because of Caddy's and Dilsey's attitudes toward him, and
in an opposite way because of Jason's, Benjy is from the
beginning a sympathetic character. But a natural compassion
for his helplessness should not cause us to assume he offers
a final way out of the dilemma inherent in the Compson heritage. Benjy is and remains "de Lawd's chile," as Dilsey
means the phrase—an idiot from birth. Like all idiots, he
cannot avoid even the common hazards of life; he is incapable of speech, and the sounds he does make appear
to be "nothing. Just sound" (303). The initial objective
description of his physical appearance in the last section
does not compromise with a romantic or sentimental view
of him nor is it influenced overtly by his symbolic and
thematic functions in the novel:

> Luster entered, followed by a big man who appeared to have
> been shaped of some substance whose particles would not or did
> not cohere to one another or to the frame which supported it.
> His skin was dead looking and hairless [Dilsey's and Luster's

skin, described in the preceding paragraph, had "a rich, lustrous quality"]; dropsical too, he moved with a shambling gait like a trained bear. His hair was pale and fine. It had been brushed smoothly down upon his brow like that of children in daguerro-types. His eyes were clear, of the pale sweet blue of cornflowers, his thick mouth hung open, drooling a little. (290)

The last scene of the novel, where Benjy bellows in "horror; shock; agony eyeless, tongueless; just sound" (335), leaves the reader with a picture of Benjy in his full idiocy.

Since it is through this character, this idiot, that the reader is introduced to the novel, obviously some license must be taken in the presentation of his interior world. Faulkner's technique in Benjy's section is geared to the solution of problems inherent in the story itself. He achieves his plot of thematic suspense and renders his subject by disallowing the objective portrait of Benjy its independent force. By the time one comes upon the objective presentation of Benjy, so much has happened that the narrator's suggestion that Benjy's wailing "might have been all time and injustice and sorrow become vocal for an instant" (303-04) or that it was "the grave hopeless sound of all voiceless misery under the sun" (332), does not seem strained, for Benjy's wailing has consistently occurred at just those points in the story where injustice, hopelessness, sorrow, and misery are manifest.

Since a strict verisimilitude in the rendering of his consciousness would produce such incoherence that not even an aesthetic gain could be made, Faulkner renders Benjy's interior life in coherent language. In order to relay the feel, the texture, of Benjy's experience, he sometimes allows him the use of comparison (Caddy smells like trees), of weak contrast ("the flower tree by the parlor window wasn't dark, but the thick trees were" [65]), and even, in rare instances, of generalization ("then the dark began to go in smooth, bright shapes, like it always does, even when Caddy says that I have been asleep" [94]). Often Benjy's language is burdened with connotations far outside of his own understanding, such as in his phrase "trying to say" (70-71, 72), an extremely powerful phrase, since his inarticulateness is his most pathetic quality. There is a subtle order in the events he recalls, and in scope they are restricted to the crucial ones: those surrounding Caddy's sexual growth and behavior, deaths in the family, the changing of his name, his attempt to attack the passing girls, the ritual of the graveyard visits, scenes showing Jason's dealings with Miss Quentin, Luster's tender although childish management of an idiot, and Dilsey's sacrificial love.

Benjy, in other words, is not an idiot in the clinical sense of the word. His monologue is flatly incredible from a naïvely realistic point of view, but perfectly convincing in its metaphorical similitude. To this extent, Faulkner's detractors, early and late, are perfectly right in saying that Benjy's section, if not the whole novel, is a tour de force. One might make a case for Quentin's articulateness since he is an effete intellectual par excellence; but the reader's initial disposition to suspend disbelief is taxed by Faulkner's attempt to render the feel and texture of an idiot's world. More than this, Faulkner, who is after all building a story, cannot even live consistently by the license he has taken in rendering Benjy's world in language. For the most part Benjy is capable of describing events accurately, but at times Faulkner must disallow even this. Consequently, *"the shaking went down the tree"* (93) and ran across the meadow. Benjy need not say this. He knows it is Miss Quentin and normally would have said so, and a careful reader would know it anyway from the 1928 scene in the swing. But Faulkner must protect his story; his plot of theme cannot come full circle until the presentation of the other major characters is complete. Thus, he cannot allow the reader to know clearly at this point that it is Miss Quentin coming down the tree.

Only when we know fully of Benjy's and Quentin's and Jason's and Dilsey's relationships to one another and to Caddy can we be properly informed of the details of action and meaning.

When caution has been taken to keep Benjy's idiocy from being lost from view, certain aesthetic and thematic facts remain to establish him as a carrier of the novel's positive theme. That he functions mainly as a contrast to Quentin is seen not only by the fact that both are concerned primarily with the same period, but also by the fact that in many ways they seem to share the same reality, even responding often in apparently the same way to that reality.

Images of obliquity—shadow, reflection, slanting, ascent and descent—fill Benjy's section too. Like Quentin, he sees his shadow walk as he walks (65) and even notices that his shadow is higher on the fence than Luster's (24). He marks "a bird slanting and tilting" (24) and "the sun slanting on the broad grass" (70), sees *"slanting holes"* in the barn roof *"full of spinning yellow"* (32) (Quentin sees the "spinning sky" [134] reflected in the water), notes ascent and descent as he goes to the Patterson's with Caddy or walks from the branch to the house, and records the sensations of drunkenness in terms of obliquity. Mirrors are prominent in his section also. Jason and Caddy fight in the mirror (83); there are two fires, one in his mother's room and one in the mirror (80); as his angle of vision changes, fires appear and disappear in mirrors. In the library there is "the dark tall place on the wall" where the mirror once stood, and Benjy says "it was like a door, only it wasn't a door" (79-80).

Many of the images are the same, yet the reality they imply is only superficially coincident with Quentin's; the images occur to Quentin and Benjy with a fundamentally different feel. The images of obliquity are for Quentin the entire content of his experience; they indicate the limits of his interpretation of reality in that final stage where being itself becomes his private problem. Only by an overinterpretation of reality, the product of a precious intellectualization where an object is less real than its shadow, where events reflected and reflected upon are more actual than they are in their full immediacy, is Quentin able to maintain a coherent experience at all.

While Quentin is too discriminating, too reflective and interpretative, Benjy is apparently, but only apparently, not discriminating at all. The sections subsequent to his bear out that the events he recalls are in fact the crucial ones in the family history, and close inspection shows that they are fairly well ordered in the period between 1898 and 1910. As they are initially rehearsed for the reader, they do appear to be without sequence, form, or meaningful progression because many of the clues to their sequence become evident only as the narration progresses. Benjy does not show discrimination, however, at the level of the immediate. He confuses the "caddie!" called out by the golfers with his sister. The experience of snagging on a fence in 1928 becomes identified with a similar experience in about 1902. Indeed, just such associations trigger his recollections and provide the rationale for his train of thought. It is through his entire character and not in his mental processes that he reflects the action in which Quentin is involved. All events flooding into his consciousness are immediate, those of the past as well as those of the present. Benjy does, of course, interpret, but minimally. By what his consciousness selects to notice, by how he notices it (confusing smell and feel or sight and sound, for example), or by his different overt responses (such as wailing or clawing at the gate or pulling Caddy's dress), he interprets. But without such fundamental interpretative responses there could be no narration at all.

The most salient contrast between Benjy's recollections and Quentin's is in their reliability. For all of Benjy's idiocy, he can be absolutely trusted, within the limits of a consistent pattern, as a reporter of his sensations. When he eats, Luster's or Caddy's or Versh's hand comes up to him; after Dilsey gives him a flower, "her hand went away" (30); when he burns his hand, "I put my hand out to where the fire had been. . . . My hand jerked back and I put it in my mouth and Dilsey caught me. I could still hear the clock between my voice. . . . My voice was going loud every time" (78). When he hears insect sounds, "the grass was buzzing" (65), and as he walks toward the branch, he does not come upon a ditch, but the ditch comes upon him; "the ditch came up out of the buzzing grass" (54). Descriptions of his drunkenness at Caddy's wedding and Damuddy's funeral are completely from his own sensational reference. Benjy tells us that he *"could hear the roof"* (85) rather than the rain on the roof, "could smell the bright cold" (26), telescoping here smell and sight and touch, and that his *"hands could see the slipper and I squatted there, hearing it getting dark"* (91). When he says that Caddy smelled like trees, we have no doubt that she did, especially when we find him perfectly consistent, for Caddy wet "smelled like trees in the rain" (38). Since his reports of the impingement of physical reality upon him are so consistent and psychologically credible, his statements about less concrete sensations, given with the same matter-of-factness, tend also to be convincing. He can *"smell the sickness"* in his mother's room, *"it was a cloth folded on Mother's head"* (80); when Damuddy dies, he can smell the death (53); and Dilsey claims he can smell the imminent catastrophe of Miss Quentin's robbery (304).

Quentin's experience of the events between 1898 and 1910 is much more rich, complex, and various than Benjy's, even though it receives the distortion of his private sensibility. But for the very reason of their simplicity, Benjy's responses function as a quick moral index to events. When Caddy, at the age of fourteen, uses perfume, she no longer smells like trees; Benjy cries and her power over him is lost. When she washes off the perfume, he goes to her: " 'Did you find Caddy again.' she said. 'Did you think Caddy had run away.' Caddy smelled like trees" (61). At another time, when she is with Charlie in the swing, she loses her tree smell but regains it by washing her mouth. At her wedding, Benjy, though drunk, moans and claws the wall and says that she no longer smells like trees. The most prominent events, some of which have just been noted, center around Caddy's sexual corruption, but Benjy's responses to Jason's activity on Easter Sunday and to the church services the same day, or to any scene of violent feeling, show that throughout he plays the role of refractor and, by his reaction, of moral judge.

His role as moral judge, of course, is clearly dramatic rather than intellectual. As a matter of dramatic fact he does function as the family's conscience, but by no means can his reaction to events be generalized beyond the novel. As an idiot, with the mental age of three, he is as ego-centered in his own way as is Quentin. If viewed from outside the dramatic context, his reactions to Caddy's sexual experiments and to scenes of violent feeling show a purely selfish distress over any threat to his stable, ordered world. Benjy has found security in a certain order of life and, as in the novel's last scene, throws a three-year-old's temper tantrum with a thirty-three-year-old's bellow when his security is threatened by change.

Benjy functions as a moral touchstone in another way. Many of the main characters of the novel can be ranged according to how they respond to him. It is significant that Jason, Miss Quentin, Uncle Maury, and Mrs. Compson are repelled by him or hostile toward him, while Dilsey treats him with tenderness. It is, of course, Caddy whose character is most illuminated by her response to Benjy. There is no doubt about her love for him and her sensitivity to his love. Mr. Compson's belief that her sexual life is merely an instance of natural human folly is shown to be superficial more by the agony through which Caddy goes in the face of Benjy's judgments than by anything else. Caddy's power over him varies with her moral purity. When she plans to marry and move away it is of Benjy's welfare in her absence that she first thinks. The two scenes, juxtaposed in Benjy's section, showing Caddy and Miss Quentin entertaining their suitors in the swing point up by contrast their attitudes toward him. Caddy's scene ends with "I wont. . . . I wont anymore, ever. Benjy. Benjy," while Miss Quentin threatens to tell Dilsey, *"You old crazy loon. . . . I'm going to make her whip you good"* (67). Miss Quentin knocks the lighted match from her beau's hand, not out of compassion for Benjy, but because "he'll beller all day" (68).

Because Benjy's love for Caddy is not finally efficacious, because his moral judgments, given dramatically, upon the events of the Compson household do little more than heighten their poignancy, one cannot claim that his character offers a solution to the utterly skeptical view implied by the negative theme. Still, Benjy's presence in the novel could not serve to intensify the Compson tragedy did not he in some way and to some degree embody a real alternative. That is, powerless though he may finally be as an agent of the action (his judgments are not enough to deter Caddy's impulses), he is nonetheless powerful as its refractor, as a character through whom the events appear in a light different from the perspective given in Quentin's consciousness. This is not to say that Benjy has all the same problems as Quentin, or that he solves them in a more meaningful way. Benjy's inability to reason, to see implications, to regard events in total context, means that in the last analysis his effectiveness as a carrier of the positive theme is quite limited in a rational sense, and his self-centered idiocy effectively undercuts any tendency the reader might have to exalt his nonrationality.

Symbolically, however, there is wisdom in Benjy's senses; he clearly points the way, indicates the direction, embodies the fundamental elements of the solution to the problems posed by the negative theme. For example, unlike Quentin, he associates Caddy with the life-suggesting trees, not with the sex- and death-suggesting water. Water cleanses Caddy (of perfume, of Charlie's taint) for Benjy. He loves Caddy and firelight, while Quentin associates fire with a private hell in which he and Caddy expiate a sin they cannot commit. Benjy too has a demand for order, and if it is limited, it is at least an order present and meaningful, not lost and devitalized. His birthday does not fall on the day of resurrection and hope, but neither does it fall on the day of crucifixion and despair. These are slight evidences upon which to pin the presence of an affirmative theme, but they are nonetheless there as symbolic contrasts. Mere love, sheer revulsion from evil, is not enough, but it is a place from which to start. Like Jason, Benjy simply "does not have it" in fact, but unlike Jason, he does have it in principle.

VII

It is in the character of Dilsey that the greatest evidence for a fulfilling meaning in experience lies. Again one must be careful not to overstate the case, for we do not have the advantage with Dilsey of the intimate revelation of character possible in the monologue. And the section in which we are given the most sustained look at her focuses also upon Jason's pursuit of Miss Quentin. Yet Section IV is Dilsey's in an important way; there Jason's actions do not stand without direct and powerful dramatic commentary. His pursuit of Miss Quentin occurs at the same time and in direct contrast to the Easter service. Reverend Shegog's vision, shared by Dilsey, of "de ricklickshun en de blood of de Lamb" (311) differs generically from Jason's "Am I bleeding much? . . . Am I bleeding? . . . Look at my head. . . . I thought I was bleeding" (326-27) and from Quentin's "the tie was spoiled too, but then niggers. Maybe a pattern of blood he could call that the one Christ was wearing" (190). And Jason's tormented frustration is balanced by the spiritual contentment of Dilsey's "annealment" in "the blood of the remembered Lamb" and Benjy's "rapt . . . sweet blue gaze" (313).

More than any other character, Dilsey exemplifies a realistic living in the face of the event's full force. This realism is her "truth," the way she deals with experience to elicit its value. "I does de bes I kin" (332) shows an endurance in historical time, not in fear or frantic hostility, but with a serenity stemming from a realistic confidence in life. In the face of a Quentin-like taunting by nine-year-old Caddy, who tries to cast doubt upon her identity and her significance as a creature in the scheme of things, Dilsey remains composed:

> My name been Dilsey since fore I could remember and it be Dilsey when they's long forgot me.
>
> How will they know it's Dilsey, when it's long forgot, Dilsey, Caddy said.
>
> It'll be in the Book, honey, Dilsey said. Writ out.
>
> Can you read it, Caddy said.
>
> Wont have to, Dilsey said. They'll read it for me. All I got to do is say Ise here. (77)

Hers is "the heart's truth" (GDM, 260), in Isaac McCaslin's phrase. She need not "know" in some intellectual sense; her conviction is "beyond the need for words" (310). Isaac says that God's Book—which can be taken to be the whole creation and our experience of it as well as the Bible and the Book in which Dilsey knows her name is written—was not written to be read by the intellect, "by what must elect and choose, but by the heart, not by the wise of the earth because maybe they dont need it or maybe the wise no longer have any heart, but by the doomed and lowly of the earth who have nothing else to read with but the heart. Because the men who wrote his Book for Him were writing about truth" (*GDM*, 260). While Isaac's statement creates problems of its own, the thrust of it is true to what Faulkner has dramatized in the figure of Dilsey. In her character we are pushed beyond the rational, not to deny it, but to affirm that it is neither all of life nor enough of life. Unlike Quentin who must have unambiguous intellectual assurance of the meaning of every event, and unlike Jason who judges each event by its potential threat to his self-image, Dilsey is like St. Augustine, willing to postpone the assurance of knowledge, to wait for "the Lawd's own time" (44, 45). At such a time, says Augustine, "it will be seen that God's judgements are utterly righteous. . . . Then, too, it will become manifest by what righteous judgement of God it is determined that so many, in fact almost all, of the righteous judgements of God are concealed from human perception and understanding."[13]

The concept of time implied by Dilsey's response to events is realistic in the sense in which John Marsh describes the Biblical understanding of time as "realistic" as opposed to "chronological." "For modern Western man," he says— and Quentin is a case in point—"the emphasis is on the 'chronological': he thinks of time as something to be measured, measured by a clock."[14] The New Testament makes use of *chronos*, of course, and so does Dilsey, in her own way, with her one-handed clock:

[13] *The City of God Against the Pagans*, trans. William Chase Greene, The Loeb Classical Library, VI (Cambridge, Mass.: Harvard University Press, 1960), Bk. XX, Ch. ii, 257-59.
[14] "Time, Season," in *A Theological Word Book of the Bible*, ed. Alan Richardson (New York: The Macmillan Co., 1950), p. 258.

> Dilsey went out. She closed the door and returned to the kitchen. The stove was almost cold. While she stood there the clock above the cupboard struck ten times. "One oclock," she said aloud, "Jason aint comin home. Ise seed de first en de last," she said, looking at the cold stove, "I seed de first en de last." (316)

But, Marsh continues, the great contribution of the New Testament, and its major emphasis, is *kairos. Kairos* is "realistic" time, the right time, "time of opportunity and fulfillment" (258). Significant times, in other words, "are known by their contents and . . . their content is always in nature and in history, endowed by God" (259). This is Dilsey's time, in nature and history and under divine control:

> Thus the whole of history, past, present and future, consists of times that are all, in the Psalmist's phrase, 'in God's hands' (Ps. 31.15). But in that history, two times especially can be discerned —the time of God's making of his people, and the time of his remaking of them. In the meantime all that happens, for weal or woe, is under divine control. (260)

Dilsey's vision of the first and the last can be interpreted in a variety of ways—the Alpha and Omega of the Christ event she has just experienced in church, the beginning of the Compson misery in Mr. Compson and its end in Jason, the first of the various Compson children (she reared them all) and their final pathetic states, the first and the last in the metaphorical sense that all chronological events are in the hands of God whose sacrifice she has just rehearsed, or, in terms of their exemplification of human virtues, the paradoxical reversal of the first who shall be last (Jason) and the last who shall be first (Benjy).

Dilsey's refraction of the Jason–Miss Quentin action is effective because she identifies herself with the situation. Her offering of herself as a substitute sacrifice in the scene where Jason threatens Miss Quentin with his belt is perfectly natural and spontaneous because she sees herself as implicated:

"Hit me, den," she says, "ef nothin else but hittin somebody wont do you. Hit me," she says.

"You think I wont?" I says.

"I dont put no devilment beyond you," she says. (203)

This devilment is something she knows she and her children share as human beings with the Compsons. Luster, a child still, has not yet learned this:

"Dese is funny folks. Glad I aint none of em."

"Aint none of who?" Dilsey said. "Lemme tell you somethin, nigger boy, you got jes es much Compson devilment in you es any of em. Is you right sho you never broke dat window?" (292)

Dilsey makes no claim to virtue beyond others. "I does de bes I kin . . . Lawd knows dat" (332) and "I cant do but one thing at a time" (287) are humble self-criticisms which at the same time acknowledge the historical limitations under which she works. And work she does, toiling heavily up and down the stairs in answer to Mrs. Compson's steady, inflectionless, and incessant calling, supervising the routines of meals and the bedding down of the children. *"Hush your mouth. . . . Sit down, honey. . . .* When you going to get done eating, boy" (90); "Hush. . . . You all get undressed, now" (92); "All right, here I is. I'll fill hit soon ez I git some hot water" (283); "You hush yo mouf. . . . You git Benjy started now en I beat yo head off" (300); "Y'all come on en eat. . . . Y'all kin g'awn en eat" (317); "Hush. Dilsey got you. . . . Luster, honey, . . . Will you think about yo ole mammy en drive dat surrey right?" (332)—these are the phrases of the daily routine in which she fulfills the role of the mother for the entire household.

They are phrases of love and concern, of direct involvement in the daily life, and they stand in striking contrast to the nominal mother's self-pitying bids for attention: "Why did you come in here. To give him some excuse to worry me again" (27); "It seems to me you all could furnish me with a driver for the carriage once a week. It's little enough I ask, Lord knows" (29); "Why are you teasing him. . . . Why wont you let him alone, so I can have some peace" (60); "What reason did Quentin have? . . . It cant be simply to flout and hurt me. Whoever God is, He would not permit that. I'm a lady" (315). Dilsey tells Mr. Compson to go to bed—"I bet you aint had a full night's sleep since you lef"—while Mrs. Compson's reproach to her husband in the same scene is "Look at me, I suffer too" (217). Dilsey buys a cake with her own money for Benjy's birthday (Jason counts every egg), and Mrs. Compson interprets her kindness as ignorant laziness: "Do you want to poison him with that cheap store cake" (79). To the new baby, Miss Quentin, Dilsey responds with "Who else gwine raise her 'cep me?" (216) while Mrs. Compson, who has failed to function as a mother to her own children "would thank God" if Miss Quentin "could grow up never to know that she had a mother" (217). And years later, Miss Quentin, "damn near naked" (202) before Jason's cruelty, cries, "Dilsey, I want my mother" (203).

"I like to know whut's de hurt in lettin dat po chile see her own baby" (225); "Now, now . . . he aint gwine so much as lay his hand on you while Ise here" (203); "Dilsey make your hand stop hurting in just a minute" (78); *"Now, now. . . . He aint going to bother you no more"* (89); *"Sit down, honey. . . . He ought to be shamed of hisself, throwing what aint your fault up to you"* (90); "You all be quiet now, you hear. . . . Go to sleep, now" (93); "Now, now, . . . Whut kin happen? I right here" (298). Such are Dilsey's words, falling in scene after scene, lending to the novel her solid presence, cajoling, threatening, comforting, giving endlessly of herself to counter the very events which undo the Compsons. Benjy bellows, Mrs. Compson whines, Jason complains of his victimization, Quentin commits suicide in despair, Caddy becomes a whore, Miss Quentin runs off with a pitchman who is already under indictment for bigamy, and Mr. Compson drinks himself to death while giving cynical pronouncements on life ("created by disease, within putrefaction, into decay" [63]) and claiming that "no battle is ever won. . . . They are not even fought. The field only reveals to man his own folly and despair, and victory is an illusion of philosophers and fools" (95). Dilsey experiences it all, from the beginning to the end, and endures. Neither a philosopher nor a fool, she not only fights the battle but wins it. She, with Benjy, stands as a contradiction, a denial that the responses of the Compsons are inevitable and unavoidable. Her judgment upon them is in her whole character, her whole life, for they could have made the same response to the events which she made, a response of love, self-sacrifice, compassion, and pity.

The response of love is not only her greatest comment upon the Compsons, but it is also her way of actively engaging the evil of their situation. For Dilsey does, as the others do not, attack the basic situation with the tools at hand. Benjy responds in principle in the same way as Dilsey, but is atrophied in fact by the limitations of his psyche. In Dilsey we have the fully developed response of the compassionate human being and the most effective carrier of the affirmative theme. Her singing, "repetitive, mournful and plaintive, austere" (286), is symbolic of the realistic courage which allows her, in the face of the most devastating evidences of meaninglessness, to find "de power en de glory" (313).

For his Appendix commentary on Dilsey, Faulkner lets a sentence of two words suffice: "they endured" (22). He thereby refers through her to the whole Negro community of *The Sound and the Fury*. Dilsey does not stand alone as a carrier of the positive theme, but she is the most representative because she is given the most complete portrayal. Quentin gained some wisdom when New England taught him that a Negro was "a sort of obverse reflection of the white people he lives among" (105). "They come into white people's lives," he says, "in sudden sharp black trickles that isolate white facts for an instant in unarguable truth like under a microscope" (189). It is in this way that Dilsey and the other Negroes come into the novel, to illuminate "in unarguable truth" the alternate response to the facts of experience, to embody the positive theme that experience can exhibit a saving and meaningful essence.

The Sound and the Fury is not a novel calculated to glorify the Negro or to show him to be different from anyone else. But the Negro does have an important and almost unique function in the novel. Dilsey's admonition to the children to "tune up" (46) is balanced by T. P. and Luster's "Hum up, Queenie" (30, 333) and by Louis Hatcher's "Hum awn, dawg" (134). In subtle and indirect ways, all of the Negroes refract the white people among whom they live, changing by obversion their negative implications about the facts of experience into positive ones. Old Job, Luster, Versh, T. P., Roskus, Frony, Louis Hatcher, but most of all Dilsey witness in their character that under these historical conditions of decay and violence, in this circumstance of a family without love and honor, at this time in the modern world, and in this way—by love and forbearance—it is possible to experience life at once realistically and meaningfully. The facts of experience can carry their own warrant of value.

The Theological Center of
Absalom, Absalom!

I

"SOMEWHERE in the heart of experience," says
Darley, Lawrence Durrell's narrator in *Justine*, "there is an
order and a coherence which we might surprise if we were
attentive enough, loving enough, or patient enough."[1]
Absalom, Absalom! is Faulkner's attentive, loving, and patient exploration into the heart of experience, past and
present, to trap its meaning in an aesthetic mold. Here again
he is on theological center, probing reality imaginatively
through multiple perceptions to lay bare its order and character and to render the meaning carried in the face of it by
the facts of experience.

The initial task, and the final one also, in an analysis of
Absalom, Absalom! is to determine accurately the controlling
function of its narrative method. This is not to say that the
novel marks a radical departure in method. Reality is rendered symbolically and mimetically; events and meanings,
actions and symbols are fused through character. Some of the
narrative devices are, however, in many ways singular. The
final vision of reality is not Quentin's. It is a larger reality
in the context of which the one created by Quentin's imagination is made credible. Sutpen's history is only what Quentin
is able, with the help of others, to make of it, and what
he can make of it is conditioned by the limitations of that

[1] (New York: E. P. Dutton & Co., 1957), p. 221.

sensibility already presented in *The Sound and the Fury*. Quentin reconstructs the history in such a way that it posits a reality infected with a meaning peculiar to him. The imaginative act by which he creates the story is of the same order as the imaginative act of the author who shows Quentin unable to understand the meaning of his own creation. With Quentin as with the author, the imaginative process begins with the creation of the facts themselves; even the final explanation of the central mystery in Sutpen's story (why Sutpen's design failed) is really only an intuitive judgment on Quentin's part of what "must have been" and has no foundation in an "objective" fact provided by the author.

Special attention must be paid to point of view, focus of character, and focus of interest, because in their complex relationship lies the key both to the nature of the final reality posited and to the kind of meaning implied by experience of that reality. Attention is initially forced upon point of view, since the question of reliability arises almost immediately for the reader when with Quentin he is in the presence of Rosa's nearly disembodied voice as she conjures with the obvious distortion of intense frustration and hatred a demonic image of Sutpen from "old ghost-times" (*AA, 9*). After some relief from ambiguity at the beginning of Chapter II, Mr. Compson's memory narrative begins to dominate. Its initial tone of authority quickly vanishes; his tired skepticism embellished with a seedy sophistication evidences the character of his own distortions.

When Quentin and Shreve take up the narrative, again private interests determine both subject matter and interpretation. Their guesses about what must have been are based upon facts which Mr. Compson (in much of his narration) and Rosa (although she alone of the narrators knew Sutpen well during his lifetime) did not have before them, but the reader's discovery of this fact only undermines the reliability of Mr. Compson and Rosa as narrators without giving him confidence in Quentin and Shreve. Shreve and Quentin's relationship as northerner and southerner, novice and expert, their "youthful shame of being moved" (280) in each other's presence, and their great sense of personal identification with Bon and Henry charge the latter half of the novel with an emotional intensity which does little to enhance the reader's comfort about the reliability of their dual narrative.

Nor is there significant relief from ambiguity of fact and meaning in the implied author's contribution. At few points can the reader assume with certainty that he is getting the facts of Sutpen's life, and at fewer points can he rely upon the author for direct interpretation of either Sutpen's or Quentin's story. The author is usually less than omniscient and more than an observer; he describes outward, physical setting, gesture, and speech but intrudes usually with more than surmise and less than omniscience into the thoughts, motives, and states of feeling of the other narrators and the characters. With Quentin, Shreve, Mr. Compson, and Rosa he indulges in guesswork, using words such as "maybe," "probably," and "perhaps" to weaken further the insecurity of the reader's knowledge.

Into this narrative maze the reader is drawn and compelled to participate in the unraveling of the story. Until the end of the novel he shares Bon's feeling that *"you cannot know yet whether what you see is what you are looking at or what you are believing"* (314). But he does have one advantage. His distance—moral, intellectual, and emotional—from Sutpen's story diminishes less rapidly than that of any of the narrators because he sees them correcting one another to such an extent that final judgment can be withheld until the end of the novel. Only when all of the various sensibilities have presented their "facts," have assigned causes appropriate to the facts, and have shown their reactions to them does the reader feel obliged to make the crucial choices regarding the meanings carried by those facts. During the experience of reading, the reader has before him only the process of the creation of the story through recollection, interpretation, and imagination. When the story is over, the fluid images of the tale solidify, enabling the reader to form his judgments on the basis of the norms rendered by the novel as a whole.

Attention to the problem of point of view forces a formal distinction between the tale told and the telling of it, since, like *The Sound and the Fury,* the novel presents two main actions. The present-tense action is Quentin's telling, or being told and remembering. Backstage is the history of Sutpen, never clear, always fluid, known only as it filters through several sensibilities into the tale being told. This means that the novel's focus of character is divided between Quentin and Sutpen. The image of Sutpen, the central figure of the tale told, emerges as Mr. Compson's image, or Rosa's, or Shreve's, but finally Quentin's.

So it is that investigation of point of view leads to the problem of focus of character. That Sutpen's real story is never known is the clue here: there is no single true story apart from its interpretation. The events of his life take on meaning as causes are assigned to them according to the penchant, the personal history, and the intellectual bias of the several narrators. The novel is not history, not even in form, but art; that is, it records the events of Sutpen's life not in the order in which they took place but in the order in which they become significant in the recollection of the characters telling the story, and especially in Quentin's experience of recreation.[2] Had Faulkner wanted simply to give

---

[2] This distinction between history and art comes from *Justine,* p. 115: "What I most need to do is to record experiences, not in the order in which they took place—for that is history—but in the order in which they first became significant for me."

the story of Thomas Sutpen, the character-narrators would
be superfluous. What he has given indicates that his purpose
is more comprehensive than a history of Sutpen or even a
history of the Deep South. The way in which he has given
Sutpen's story indicates that the greatest tool for his purpose
is the character of Quentin Compson—Quentin, because it is
with him that the book opens, in his presence that the narrative proceeds, and with him and his reaction to the total
impact of the imaginatively constructed history that the book
closes. What the backstage action both is and means is how
it occurs to Quentin; its meaning as well as its character lies
in the context and manner of its emergence—the intellectual, moral, and emotional present in which it comes to life—
and this context is finally Quentin himself.

This is Quentin's story as much as, and in a different way
from, Sutpen's. The present-tense action gives us Quentin's
reaction to the Sutpen saga. In the dramatic detail of Quentin's confronting the past, it provides a long footnote on the
character and content of that southern past in the face of
which he forged his final truant strategy. The reader is forced
to focus upon whatever it is in Sutpen's story qua Quentin's
creation that holds such fascination for Quentin and, indeed,
binds the two actions—the tale told and the telling of it—
to render one effect. That is, the reader's focus of interest is
upon the novel's theme, its import, its meaning, not simply
for Quentin but for himself, although he arrives at its theme
through the way the novel as a whole evaluates the evidence
presented by Quentin's creation.

It is significant that when Quentin's eye turns to the past
it rests upon one who is not an exemplar of the aristocratic
tradition with which *The Sound and the Fury* supposedly
showed him to be the most concerned. Malcolm Cowley once
pointed out that Sutpen was not an aristocrat of the Comp-
son-Sartoris-McCaslin order, but one of the "new men," the
huge plantation owners who, with the aristocrats, "were

determined to establish a lasting social order on the land they had seized from the Indians (that is, to leave sons behind them)."[3] Just how valid Cowley's distinction is and just what its implications are need to be made clear, since it is crucial in two ways for an understanding of the novel. It is crucial first of all for Quentin, and, in the second place, for Faulkner.

When Quentin is asked by his Harvard contemporaries to tell about the South, he responds with the story of Sutpen. In some way, Sutpen's story holds for him the key to the whole southern experience. If he could explain Sutpen, if he could account for the fact that a Sutpen could exist and that he could not but fail of his "design," he could also explain the South. As the story develops, it becomes apparent that he cannot simply contrast traditional and untraditional men. Though wanting desperately to believe that the distinction to which Cowley points is valid, he senses that Sutpens are possible because of something in the traditional society itself. In order to explain the one he must illuminate the other. Quentin never becomes clear about either; he grasps intellectually the difference between the tradition's ideal claim and Sutpen's untraditional actions, but reacts only with violent emotion (even with a physical spasm) to his vague sense that in Sutpen's story the actual tradition is dramatized, stripped of its ideal vision. Rather than explaining either Sutpen or the aristocrat, he judges both and in such a way that neither offers any hope for meaning in his own experience. At the end of his story he admits failure. The question is posed again: "it's something my people haven't got," Shreve says, "What is it? something you live and breathe in like air?" "You cant understand it. You would have to be born there," Quentin replies—this after three hundred and fifty pages of trying to understand it himself. "Do you understand it?" Shreve asks again, and

[3] "Introduction to *The Portable Faulkner*," in *Three Decades*, p. 102.

Quentin says, " 'I dont know. . . . Yes, of course I under-stand it.' . . . [And] after a moment Quentin said: 'I dont know' " (361-62).

The novel does not leave us, however, only with Quentin's despair. It is legitimate to look upon the novel, taken in its total performance, as a witness to Faulkner's own judgment of the southern past. Here—and Quentin should not be con-fused with Faulkner—both the tradition and the modern world are tested in an aesthetic mold for their truth, the insight they yield into the value and meaning of any man's experience. It is wrong to assume that because Faulkner allows his investigation to proceed under Quentin's limited sensibility the book's illumination of the past is only as clear as Quentin's understanding of it. Quentin himself is under investigation in the novel. Faulkner's total fictional strategy is, in a limited sense, the same as Quentin's. He too uses the story of one of the new men to illuminate the inadequacy of both traditional and modern assessments of reality. But Faulkner becomes clear about the implications of the evi-dence Quentin presents, while Quentin remains confused. Faulkner's look at the past is aesthetically controlled to allow a deliberate judgment from a point of view wider than Quentin's. When we understand the character of the aes-thetic judgment, we understand the character of Faulkner's theological center in this novel. We will look first at Quen-tin's attempt to deal with the Sutpen story.

II

The distinction between traditional and untradi-tional societies Quentin wants to bring to Sutpen's story is explained, in another context, by Allen Tate, who contrasts the relationship within each of them between the economic and moral orders. Using the word "morality" to mean "responsibility to a given set of conditions," he finds the traditional society to be one which hands on "a moral conception of man in relation to the material of life," and the untraditional society, of which our modern society is a prime example, to be "hostile to the perpetuation of a moral code" because the "economic system can be operated efficiently regardless of the moral stature of the men who operate it." Traditional men "are making their living all the time, and affirming their humanity all the time,"[4] while modern men "are no longer capable of defining a human objective" and "capitulate from their human role to a series of pragmatic conquests" (301).

The Unvanquished provides a short account of Sutpen from one of his contemporaries who stood in the aristocratic tradition. Bayard Sartoris, in unequivocal terms, says of Sutpen:

> He was underbred, a cold ruthless man who had come into the country about thirty years before the War, nobody knew from where except Father said you could look at him and know he would not dare to tell. He had got some land and nobody knew how he did that either, and he got money from somewhere . . . and built a big house and married and set up as a gentleman. Then he lost everything in the War like everybody else, all hope of descendants too (his son killed his daughter's fiancé on the eve of the wedding and vanished) yet he came back home and set out singlehanded to rebuild his plantation. He had no friends to borrow from and he had nobody to leave it to and he was past sixty years old, yet he set out to rebuild his place like it used to be; they told how he was too busy to bother with politics or anything; how when Father and the other men organised the night riders to keep the carpet baggers from organising the Negroes into an insurrection, he refused to have anything to do with it. Father stopped hating him long enough to ride out to see Sutpen himself

---

[4] *On the Limits of Poetry: Selected Essays 1928-1948* (New York: The Swallow Press and William Morrow & Co., 1948), p. 303. Also found in Tate's *Collected Essays* (Denver: Alan Swallow, 1960), p. 303.

and he (Sutpen) came to the door with a lamp and did not even invite them to come in and discuss it; Father said, "Are you with us or against us?" and he said, "I'm for my land. If every man of you would rehabilitate his own land, the country will take care of itself" and Father challenged him to bring the lamp out and set it on a stump where they could both see to shoot and Sutpen would not. (255-56)

Bayard here emphasizes those aspects of Sutpen's career and character which set him apart from the aristocratic ideal: lack of breeding, ruthlessness, suspicious origin, and unwillingness to participate in accepted forms of social behavior except when there is personal advantage. Quentin's grandfather, who also knew him, is quick to point out that Sutpen, lacking a received tradition, confused shrewdness with unscrupulousness, "or maybe," General Compson says, "that was what he meant by courage" (*AA*, 250). Mr. Compson believed that Wash Jones, admittedly of the landless white class, shared with Sutpen a morality "that told him he was right in the face of all fact and usage and everything else" (287). Rosa, more ignorant than any of the narrators of the facts of Sutpen's life, yet more directly a part of it, calls him a man "with valor and strength but without pity or honor" (20). By his own confession, the sum of Sutpen's learning from the incident of the "monkey-dressed" Negro at the Virginia plantation door was that "to combat them you have got to have what they have that made them do what the man did. You got to have land and niggers and a fine house to combat them with" (238).

Sutpen and his biographers thus testify that he is set apart from the aristocrats by a lack of humanity in Tate's sense of the word. Prior to his experience at the plantation door,

he no more envied the man than he would have envied a mountain man who happened to own a fine rifle. He would have coveted the rifle, but he would himself have supported and confirmed the owner's pride and pleasure in its ownership because he could not have conceived of the owner taking such crass advantage of the luck which gave the rifle to him rather than to another as to say to other men: *Because I own this rifle, my arms and legs and blood and bones are superior to yours.* (228-29)

The incident itself came as such a shock that he figuratively crawled back into the womb (literally, a cave) to be reborn to another world of experience, because his life had contained no experience "to compare and gauge it by" (234). He was reborn to a vision of his own "innocence," for "it was like that," Sutpen said, "like an explosion—a bright glare that vanished and left nothing, no ashes nor refuse; just a limitless flat plain with the severe shape of his intact innocence rising from it like a monument" (238). He emerged from his shock with a recognition of what he took to be his destiny and his fate: he was sent to the door *so that* the Negro could affront him, *so that* he could learn what it took to combat them. In Greek fashion, his fate became an extension of his will; in vindication "of that little boy who approached that door fifty years ago and was turned away," Sutpen told Quentin's grandfather, General Compson, "the whole plan was conceived and carried forward" (274).

But the human—or inhuman—content of the Negro agent's action suffers in time from abstraction. Fifty years later "that little boy" was merely a "boy-symbol at the door," "just the figment of the amazed and desperate child" (261). Consequently, when in the figure of Bon "the forlorn nameless and homeless lost child" (267) comes fifty years later to knock at his own door, Sutpen turns him away. Because he was his son, Bon's human claim upon Sutpen was greater than Sutpen's upon the plantation owner. Quentin and Shreve believe that Bon "wanted so little" (321), just the human recognition, "just the saying of it—the physical touch even though in secret, hidden—the living touch of that flesh" (319), a touch which Rosa believes precipitates *"the fall of all the eggshell shibboleth of caste and color too"*

(139). The humanity—so little—he wanted from his father, Bon in his turn denied his own son, Velery, so that the Justice of the Peace was vexed to the symbolic question, *"What are you? Who and where did you come from?"* (203). The incident of the octoroon's photograph in Bon's wallet, however, is interpreted by Quentin to mean that he did not fail completely of humanity in his most trying moment.

Because he had all along failed to comprehend what was actually involved in his initial experience and therefore to incorporate into his design the moral integrity (expressing itself in "humanity") which supposedly gave the tradition its "unity between [man's] . . . moral nature and his livelihood,"[5] Sutpen could assign the cause of the design's collapse only to "an old mistake in fact which a man of courage and shrewdness . . . could still combat if he could only find out what the mistake had been" (*AA*, 267-68).

There are also other ways by which Sutpen is set apart from the aristocrats. Lacking the humanity they espoused and therefore unable to affirm the integrity of their total way of life, Sutpen emphasized the material side. He assumed that possession of house, land, and slaves was the entire content of the aristocrat's distinction. And one must be careful to note that he was led to this conclusion by an incident in which the tradition had not functioned according to its ideal spirit. His conclusion was correct on the basis of his evidence: "to combat them you have got to have what they have *that made them do what the man did*" (italics mine). What the man did was to act untraditionally (without the humanity), and his action was licensed by sheer economic power.

It is Drusilla of *The Unvanquished* who points up Sutpen's moral isolation from the community. When Bayard, after summarizing Sutpen's career, says, "Nobody could have more of a dream than that," Drusilla replies, "Yes. But his dream

[5] *On the Limits of Poetry*, pp. 302-03. (*Collected Essays*, pp. 302-03.)

is just Sutpen. John's [John Sartoris'] is not. He is thinking of this whole country . . ." (256). The aristocrat takes
responsibility for the entire way of life of the community,
not out of love for his fellow man, but out of a dispassionate
sense of duty. Received and handed on in the traditional
society are the automatically operative values of the entire
community (whether they are worth preserving is, at this
point, not at issue) which express themselves in the culture's unwritten mores.

Sutpen had no feeling, no automatic receptivity, for these
values. He simply recognized them where recognition of
them was pragmatic, followed social usage as long as it was
advantageous and abandoned it when it was not, maintain-
ing always an "alertness for measuring and weighing event
against eventuality, circumstance against human nature, his
own fallible judgment and mortal clay against not only
human but natural forces, choosing and discarding, compromising with his dream and his ambition" (*AA,* 53). For
example, he "marked down Miss Coldfield's father with the
same cold and ruthless deliberation with which he had
probably marked down the French architect," came to Jefferson "to find a wife exactly as he would have gone to the
Memphis market to buy livestock or slaves" (42), and
wanted a big wedding with "the full church and all the
ritual" (49) because he calculated that the success of his
design required "not the anonymous wife and the anonymous
children, but the two names, the stainless wife and the un-
impeachable father-in-law, on the license, the patent" (51).

His attitude toward his first wife and toward Bon also
involved no personal feeling about Negro blood; they were
simply not "adjunctive to the forwarding of the design"
(262). And his attitude toward women was alien to those
who stand within the received tradition. Quentin's grandfather finds it incredible that Sutpen could presume to buy
immunity from his first wife "for no other coin but justice":

"didn't the dread and fear of females which you must have drawn in with the primary mammalian milk teach you better?" (265). General Compson's incredulity is significant because the tradition's attitude toward women was fundamental to its whole spirit. As seen in *The Sound and the Fury,* the central position of women in the matriarchal society was associated with their natural function of fertility, and involved, ultimately, the tradition's vision of evil. Shreve, speaking also for Quentin, shows understanding of this when he says of Henry and Bon that "they both knew that women will show pride and honor about almost anything except love" (341). The tradition held women to be amoral, not evil but also not not evil; women were simply natural, beyond good and evil.

The features setting Sutpen apart from the tradition's ideal —his lack of humanity, his moral variance and isolation from the community, his impersonal pragmatism, his acquisitive drive, his sense of personal destiny and fate—are a large part of what Quentin senses when he says that "Sutpen's trouble was innocence" (220). To the implication of this statement we must give some attention.

In many outward respects, Sutpen would seem to exemplify rather than to contradict the tradition's Stoic rationalization. But this is true only if one takes the word "innocent" to mean something neither Quentin nor Faulkner means by it. The word cannot mean, in this context, "not guilty," for sin and guilt are not at issue; rather, it refers to Sutpen's ignorance or lack of awareness or insensitivity or, finally, lack of knowledge of the nature of things. Cleanth Brooks says that for Faulkner Sutpen's innocence is "about the nature of reality" itself.[6] The nature of things of which he is ignorant is first of all that nature of things envisioned by the tradition's theological realism which was largely Stoic. In

---

[6] "*Absalom, Absalom:* The Definition of Innocence," *The Sewanee Review,* 545.

this sense, Sutpen is innocent of both nature and human nature. This much Quentin seems to understand, but he is only vaguely aware that Sutpen is ignorant in the second place of the reality envisioned by Christian religiousness.

In a mood of "sober and quiet bemusement" (273), indicating "that he had long since given up any hope of ever understanding it" (263), Sutpen recapitulates his story for General Compson, trying to "discover that mistake which he [still] believed was the sole cause of his problem" (271). He is "fog-bound by his own private embattlement of personal morality," by a "picayune splitting of abstract hairs" (271), and will not act again until he has found out what the mistake was. In his "innocence," Quentin says, he "believed that the ingredients of morality were like the ingredients of pie or cake and once you had measured them and balanced them and mixed them and put them into the oven it was all finished and nothing but pie or cake could come out" (263). Since his morality does not root in a realistic assessment of the nature of things, he meets his defeat at the hand of forces he never realizes to be operative. The *"old impotent logic and morality which had betrayed him before," "had never yet failed to fail him"* (279-80), could only lead him to the conclusion *"that he had been right, just as he knew he had been, and therefore what had happened was just a delusion and did not actually exist"* (280) because it did not take account of the fortuitous evil with which the tradition's Stoic morality, made realistic by the cumulative concrete experience of the historical community, was geared to deal.

The tradition's morality because it was not innocent attained wisdom. By balancing the ideology of the ruling class against its experience, it attempted to allow man to live meaningfully without presuming any ultimate order of things which would guarantee the success of the enterprise. Fate was never to be coerced, and though the source and

ultimate nature of retribution remained mysterious, its inevitable manifestation at points of outrage was a social and
political fact. Sutpen's morality, because it was unrealistic,
abstract, and merely logical, obscured the concrete evil from
constant view. When its manifestations burst upon him, his
impotent logic could only produce results which to him were
"absolutely and forever incredible" (263).

III

So far, we have measured Sutpen's innocence
against the tradition's more sophisticated view of life which
required that man forego his state of innocence and take on
the risk of the human situation—at the price of possible
tragic defeat, perhaps, but even then with the possibility
of gaining a whole realm of meaningful human experience.
We must now ask how much of this Quentin sees. Certainly
we can understand how the Quentin of *The Sound and the
Fury* could interpret Sutpen from the standpoint of a puritan
moralist. Because he shows ability to appropriate at least the
rationalization of the tradition, he can pass judgment from
a puritan rather than a Stoic point of view that Sutpen was
unable to comprehend the collapse of his design as "moral
retribution," not the "sins of the father come home to roost
. . . but just a mistake" (267). But can Quentin also understand the vital spirit of the tradition, that vision of reality
and especially that feeling for the evil, or at least the
amorality, behind the face of reality which generated the
rationalization? Evidence from *The Sound and the Fury*
would indicate that he could not. Yet one does not have to
refer to that novel for a definition of Quentin's sensibility.
Within the first few pages of *Absalom, Absalom!* and with
as omniscient a voice as he ever attains, the author provides
the clue:

Quentin had grown up with that [talk about Sutpen]; the mere names were interchangeable and almost myriad. His childhood was full of them; his very body was an empty hall echoing with sonorous defeated names; he was not a being, an entity, he was a commonwealth. He was a barracks filled with stubborn back-looking ghosts still recovering, even forty-three years afterward, from the fever which had cured the disease, waking from the fever without even knowing that it had been the fever itself which they had fought against and not the sickness, looking with stubborn recalcitrance backward beyond the fever and into the disease with actual regret, weak from the fever yet free of the disease and not even aware that the freedom was that of impotence. (12)

Faulkner gives us, in short, the double fact of Quentin's southernness and his impotence as the initial condition, the *donnée* of his character. The fullest definition of his sensibility, however, is dramatic rather than descriptive. Just how deeply he is able to penetrate the tradition is measurable by the character of his solution to the problem of why Sutpen's design failed. Quentin begins his review of the story in boredom, shut up with Rosa in the "dim hot airless room" (7), asking himself if he must go through it all again. He ends obsessed, lying on his bed in the Harvard dormitory unable to sleep, jerking violently in a physical spasm, and at last lying quietly, "breathing hard but slow, his eyes wide open upon the window, thinking 'Nevermore of peace. Nevermore of peace. Nevermore Nevermore Nevermore' " (373). Between the boredom and the despair, two crucial events occur. He visits Sutpen's mansion with Rosa and he reviews Sutpen's history with Shreve.

Just what happened that September night at Sutpen's mansion is unclear except as it can be reconstructed from the evidence of its interpretation. Shreve and Quentin do not begin to glare and stare at one another and to think as one person until they come to the story of Henry and Bon (Chapter VIII). One can easily see that the incest theme

Absalom, Absalom! 117

would interest Quentin and this must account for part of his obsession. As they merge identities with Henry and Bon— "four of them and then just two—Charles-Shreve and Quentin-Henry" (334)—Quentin's identification with Henry becomes so complete that he easily assigns to Henry his own inverted puritan evaluation of incest as a strategy for attaining being by affirming the possibility of sin:

> *and Henry said 'Thank God. Thank God,'* [when Bon decided to marry Judith] *not for the incest of course but because . . . at last he could* be [emphasis mine] *something even though that something was the irrevocable repudiation of the old heredity and training and the acceptance of eternal damnation* [a shift here, as in *The Sound and the Fury*, from the Stoic orientation to an attenuated Christian one]. . . . *he could say now, 'It isn't yours nor his nor the Pope's hell that we are all going to: it's my mother's and her mother's and father's and their mother's and father's hell.'* (347)

And there are other reasons for special interest in Henry and Bon. Bon and Henry meet each other at college, one is to the other something of a foreigner, and, of course, in a simple way one might view Quentin and Shreve as two boys in a college dormitory talking about love, "creating between them, out of the rag-tag and bob-ends of old tales and talking, people who perhaps had never existed at all anywhere" (303).

But the focus of Quentin's interest is upon the reason why Henry killed Bon. Just before the setting of the novel's present-tense action shifts to the room at Harvard where Shreve and Quentin take up the narration, we are told that Quentin stops listening to Rosa's long, self-justifying monologue:

> But Quentin was not listening, because there was also something which he too could not pass—that door, the running feet on the stairs beyond it almost a continuation of the faint shot, the two women, the negress and the white girl in her underthings . . .

pausing, looking at the door, . . . as the door crashed in and the
brother stood there, hatless, with his shaggy bayonet-trimmed hair,
his gaunt worn unshaven face, his patched and faded gray tunic,
the pistol still hanging against his flank: the two of them, brother
and sister, . . . speaking to one another in short brief staccato
sentences like slaps, as if they stood breast to breast striking one
another in turn neither making any attempt to guard against the
blows.

> *Now you cant marry him.*
> *Why cant I marry him?*
> *Because he's dead.*
> *Dead?*
> *Yes. I killed him.*
> He (Quentin) couldn't pass that. (172)

Until he can "pass that door," that is, establish the motive
for Henry's murder of Bon, Quentin cannot answer the more
basic question of why Sutpen's design failed. In the last four
chapters, Quentin and Shreve piece "the rag-tag and bob-
ends of old tales and talking" together with Quentin's personal experience.

Quentin's final solution to the mystery comes by an intuitive inference of what "must have been." Rosa and
Shreve prepare us for his dependence upon such an inference.
Rosa speaks of *"a might-have-been which is more true than
truth"* (143), *"that might-have-been which is the single rock
we cling to above the maelstrom of unbearable reality"* (149-
50). Shreve, in a characteristic variation of Rosa's words,
changes the "might-have-been" to "just have to be": "there
are some things that just have to be whether they are or not,
have to be a damn sight more than some other things that
maybe are and it dont matter a damn whether they are or
not" (322). Rosa and Shreve state what in effect is the
burden of the uncertain private reality Quentin creates with
his solution to the mystery of why Henry murdered Bon and
why Bon forced him to do it, for the solution embodies not

only his judgment upon Sutpen and the tradition but also implicitly a more fundamental judgment about the nature of human experience in reality.

Prior to Quentin's solution, the explanation of the mystery passes through two stages, each explanation assuming a vague incestuous love in Henry for his sister. At first, Mr. Compson assigns the source of the trouble to Bon's legal (though not binding) marriage ceremony with his octoroon mistress. He accounts for the ceremony's importance by an emotionally credible hypothesis about Henry's provincial puritanism and by projecting onto Bon's character his own sybaritic tastes and indifferent fatalism. He admits, however, that his solution is "just incredible. It just does not explain" (100). Miss Rosa never learns the second explanation, namely that Sutpen told Henry that Bon is his half brother.

The final solution, Quentin's own, is prepared for but not unambiguously revealed at the time of his September evening journey with Rosa. Neither his grandfather nor his father had known what Sutpen meant by that "factor" which caused him to put his first wife aside. "And when your old man told it to you, you wouldn't have known what anybody was talking about if you hadn't been out there and seen Clytie. Is that right?" (274) asks Shreve. Quentin confirms his statement. Later, Shreve continues to talk about what Quentin learned from seeing Clytie:

> And she [Clytie] didn't tell you in so many words because she was still keeping that secret . . . she didn't tell you, it just came out of the terror and the fear . . . and she looked at you and you saw it was not rage but terror, and not nigger terror because it was not about herself but was about whatever it was that was upstairs, that she had kept hidden up there for almost four years; and she didn't tell you in the actual words because even in the terror she kept the secret; nevertheless she told you, or at least all of a sudden you knew— (350-51)

The question becomes, then, what did Quentin learn "all

of a sudden" from the terror in Clytie's face? The passage indicates that he learned "about whatever it was that was upstairs." However, following this passage comes an account of what Quentin and Shreve imagine to be a scene, set in Carolina in 1865, in which Sutpen reveals to Henry at last that Bon has Negro blood. This is the first time that the fact is plainly given anywhere in the book. One would think that something in his encounter with Henry led Quentin to this conclusion; yet when the scene in which Quentin discovers Henry in the upstairs room is presented (following the imagining of the Carolina scene), there is no hint that Quentin finds out anything other than that it is Henry, that he has been in Sutpen's decayed mansion for four years, and that he has come home to die.

Now, perhaps by the ranging of these scenes in the above order Faulkner expects the reader to surmise that something in Clytie's terror or in Henry's face informs Quentin that Henry shot Bon because of the threat of miscegenation. If this is the case, Faulkner is requiring that the reader make the same incredible effort of imagination that Quentin would have to make, and then he undercuts both Quentin and the reader by giving the interpretation no foundation in objective fact. Or perhaps Faulkner simply withholds the full scene from the reader. If this is the case, one can charge Faulkner with bad writing, with pointless mystification; this means, in effect, that he has accidentally or deliberately scuttled the whole novel. But we need make such a charge only if in a total reading of the novel we fail to find another and more functional reason.

One credible explanation is that Quentin's solution to the central mystery is in the present tense, that the imagining of the scene in Carolina in 1865 occurs for the first time in the present-tense scene with Shreve, just as the imagining of the rest of the story about Henry and Bon in Chapters VIII and IX occurs at Harvard with Shreve. Some features of the scene could have been imagined at no other time than the present tense. For example, Sutpen remarks to Henry that he had heard of his being wounded at the battle of Shiloh (353). That it was Henry who was wounded rather than Bon is a "fact" created for the first time by Shreve only a few pages earlier (344).

A correlate of this conclusion is that in the September, 1909, scene we are given the entire dramatic exchange between Quentin and Henry, and the scene functions chiefly as a way of removing the whole Sutpen saga from the realm of an old ghost tale. "This meeting," as Hyatt Waggoner says, "was a confrontation with a flesh-and-blood ghost. Here is proof that the past is 'real.' "[7] Quentin finally "passes that door": Henry is real to Quentin for the first time; the past is now a twentieth-century, contemporary, present-tense reality. This must be what Harvey Breit means in his introduction to the Modern Library edition of *Absalom, Absalom!* when he writes that Quentin "is made by Faulkner to be an embodiment of the presentness of the past" (vii). Faulkner makes him thus by letting him encounter Henry in the flesh. In a sense, two revelations of the fact of Bon's Negro blood occur, the first in the story told, the second in the telling of it. But only when the second revelation occurs does the imagining of the first take place; thus, in another sense there is only one revelation, and when it occurs, the whole story falls into place for Quentin and for the reader both in "fact" and in meaning.

There is some evidence, however, that Quentin has already discovered the solution—from his grandfather or when he saw Henry—by the time he talks with Shreve. He tells Shreve that his grandfather did not know "what second choice he [Sutpen] was faced with until the very last word he spoke before he got up" (272). Further, Shreve refers to what Quentin learned from Clytie as giving Quentin

[7] *William Faulkner: From Jefferson to the World*, p. 163.

understanding of what both Mr. Compson and General Compson were talking about (274). Finally, the movement of the story Shreve is building up around Henry and Bon requires that it reach a climax in the revelation of Bon's Negro blood. In whatever way one interprets the evidence, the reality of the past becomes present reality to Quentin when he meets Henry. The Carolina scene, if it is not imagined for the first time in Harvard, is imagined there with such force (partly because of its placement in the novel) that Quentin does not doubt that it is true "a damn sight more than some other things that maybe are and it dont matter a damn whether they are or not."

IV

By an act of the imagination, Quentin thus solves the mystery of why Sutpen's design fails. The character of his solution is important because it embodies a view of the past which leaves him in despair over the possibility of meaning in the present. His sensibility in this novel has the same limitations it had in *The Sound and the Fury*. Neither Sutpen (modern man) nor the tradition (Stoic man) did in fact envision a world which is meaningful in the only way he is capable of admitting it can be meaningful. This judgment remains implied rather than explicit, however, because although he can isolate intellectually the formal element which led to the destruction of both Sutpen and the tradition, his assessment of it is only emotional.

Quentin sees that Sutpen's story and the tradition judge each other. Each fails in the same respect although not for the same reason. The tradition, finding Sutpen lacking in "humanity," can explain his failure in the general terms of retributive justice. Sutpen's innocence precludes his success because it means that he is ignorant of the nature of things and especially of the fact of evil. But the tradition also fails of the same humanity. Quentin shows how Sutpen's design was born at the moment when, in the person of the Tidewater plantation owner's Negro agent, the tradition showed an image of itself divested of its humanity, an image of naked economic power. Sutpen tells General Compson that at the moment of his shock before the plantation's "white door" (232) he suddenly recognized things he had forgotten he had even remembered. A part of him seemed to "turn and rush back through the two years they had lived there . . . seeing a dozen things that had happened and he hadn't even seen them before" (229-30).

What he saw was images of himself, his sisters, and his father in attitudes of outrageous frustration, victims and agents in a dehumanizing situation they could not even describe or understand. He remembered the "flat level silent way his older sisters . . . had of looking at niggers, not with fear or dread but with a kind of speculative antagonism not because of any known fact or reason but inherited, by both white and black" (230). He thought of evening scenes at the fireside, the women's voices "calm, yet filled with a quality dark and sullen" and one of the men breaking "out into harsh recapitulation of his own worth," both men and women "talking about the same thing though it had never once been mentioned by name, as when people talk about . . . sickness without ever naming the epidemic" (230-31). He recalled throwing clods of dirt after a retreating carriage which forced him off the road, the Negro coachman shouting to his sister, who had refused to budge from the road, "the two faces beneath the parasols glaring down at his sister," and he knew "it had not been the nigger coachman that he threw at at all" (231). And finally:

> He thought of one night late when his father came home, blundered into the cabin; he could smell the whiskey even while still dulled with broken sleep, hearing that same fierce exultation,

vindication, in his father's voice: 'We whupped one of Pettibone's niggers tonight' and he roused at that, waked at that, asking which one of Pettibone's niggers and his father said he did not know, had never seen the nigger before: and he asked what the nigger had done and his father said, 'Hell fire, that goddam son of a bitch Pettibone's nigger.' He must have meant the question the same way his father meant the answer. (231)

These are images of the ultimate degradation of the human spirit, where Negro and white are set against each other by a system each fears and is corrupted to support. Sutpen knows in each case that "they (the niggers) were not it, not what you wanted to hit" (230). Nor would killing the plantation owner restore his shattered spirit. *"But I can shoot him,"* he argues to himself, "Not the monkey nigger. It was not the nigger anymore than it had been the nigger that his father had helped to whip that night" (234). The monkey-dressed Negro at the door, Quentin conjectures, was a city-born, house-bred servant, and as such was the hothouse fruit of the aristocrat's withdrawal from the land to the ballroom. The plantation owner did not plant or harvest, but "spent most of the afternoon . . . in a barrel stave hammock between two trees, with his shoes off" (227-28) and with "a special nigger to hand him his liquor and pull off his shoes that he didn't even need to wear" (229). Nor did the white superintendents work the soil, but watched the Negroes plant and harvest.

Sutpen's own career shows something of the plantation society's devolution from the source of its vitality. At the period of his life when he is most vital, he is stripped to the waist, laboring with his twenty wild West Indies Negroes to raise his mansion from the primordial mud. He catches them at the right moment by gesture or example to gain their maximum effort. When he attains his immediate ends— land, a big house, slaves, an upright wife, a son—his life reaches a plateau where he acts out a role of arrogant leisure and ostentation but without grace or heart. Of course, all along his vision and ambition is to achieve the status which represents a corruption of the traditional ideal. His most serious "mistakes" arise from the abstract character of his conception of what his design should involve. For example, his conviction that his daughter's marriage must be one free of Negro blood shows that his understanding of the tradition is purely rationalistic, since the traditional mores demanded only that the male line remain "untainted." But for all his outward similarity to the corrupt aristocrat, he remains essentially different because of his innocence. His is the innocence of any materialist from Quentin's brother Jason to Flem Snopes who tries to solve or bypass the problem of evil with will and reason devoid of love. Sutpen's failure is crucial to Quentin partly because it is the characteristic failure of modern man.

Where the tradition actually exhibited the humanity for which it stood, its Stoic strategy for investing experience with meaning was successful. But it did not sustain its own moral vision because it could not; it became, in effect though not in essence, what Sutpen never ceased to be. The tradition lost its wisdom, whereas Sutpen simply kept his innocence. Looked at in one way, the tradition's failure was the more serious, for the tradition could not plead ignorance. It failed on its own moral terms. The question posed by Quentin's reconstructed history is why Sutpen and the tradition fail in the humanity they need. Quentin despairs of an answer, despairs of man, despairs of himself. This question is answered by a sensibility that is not Quentin's, by a vision which sees what he sees but in the context of a reality allowing one to see more than he sees, by an aesthetic organization that is Faulkner's and of which the despairing Quentin is only an element.

V

Although he works under the limitations of Quentin's sensibility, in contrast to his strategy in *The Sound and the Fury*, Faulkner does not leave his own position ambiguous. He does not speak in his own voice, but, like Quentin's, his position is implied by the way the tale is told. Specifically, he presents Quentin despairing over the implications of Sutpen's and the tradition's failures but allows, in the process, an alternative to Quentin's despair to emerge from Quentin's telling of the tale, an alternative of which Quentin, because of his limitations, is not aware. Through the entire performance of the novel, Faulkner implicitly judges from what must be called a Christian humanist point of view that both Sutpen and the tradition fail because they wrongly assess the nature of reality and especially the nature of man.

In a word, they fail to recognize the "strange work" of love, as Luther called it. Paul Tillich's clarification of this notion can help us to understand the thrust of the novel's judgment:

The tension between love and justice refers basically to salvation. . . . Love destroys, as its strange work, what is against love. . . . Love, at the same time, as its own work, saves through forgiveness that which is against love. . . . How can these two works of love be one? They are one because love does not enforce salvation. . . . Love must destroy what is against love, but not him who is the bearer of that which is against love. For as a creature, he remains a power of being or a creation of love. But the unity of his will is destroyed, he is thrown into a conflict with himself, the name of which is despair, mythologically speaking, hell. Dante was right when he called even Hell a creation of the divine love. The hell of despair is the strange work that love does within us in order to open us up for its own work, justification of him who is unjust.[8]

Quentin is too limited and too close to the process Tillich describes to understand it. He shows awareness that the tradition and Sutpen fail because of something neither of them can explain, and in his dramatic reconstruction of Sutpen's story he provides evidence for what it is: the strange work of love. It is not too much to claim, I think, that this is a novel about love, just as *The Sound and the Fury* is about love. Even Quentin and Shreve sense that all of their talking and thinking previous to the Henry-Bon-Judith affair was "just so much that had to be overpassed . . . in order to overpass to love, where there might be paradox and inconsistency but nothing fault nor false" (316). The novel is about love in a sense wider than theirs and close to Tillich's, who states in theological terms what Faulkner achieves in aesthetic mode.

The Christian humanist point of view from which Faulkner judges owes a great deal to the South's Stoic vision. The tradition is no straw man for Faulkner: it represents a signal achievement. Images of rational man willing his destiny, of finite man affirming himself in the face of fate and death, are both attractive and powerful. Words such as honor and pride and courage are not hollow and "obscene" as they were for the young Hemingway of *A Farewell to Arms;* they refer to human virtues worth achieving. But Faulkner also shows the tradition's limitations. Though it was concerned with justice and its attendant virtues, it does not appear in Faulkner's picture to have concerned itself with the virtues of love. It could not have done so without abandoning its own vision, for then it would have admitted that tension to which Tillich refers as leading to the Christian notion of salvation. In other words, the tradition was Stoic rather than Christian. Salvation (and, consequently, love) is the

8 *Love, Power, and Justice* (New York: Oxford University Press, 1954), pp. 113-14.

answer to the problem of sin rather than of ignorance. The notion of sin implies that man is estranged, because of his own guilt, from his essential (rational) nature, that his reason and will cannot rescue him because they *are* his problem. The traditional and Stoic doctrine of man calls for knowledge rather than love. If there is any salvation needed, it is not rescue from sin by the justification brought by love, but resolution of ignorance by the knowledge brought by the exercise of will and reason. Man's problem is finitude, not guilt, and when things go wrong the responsibility is fate's and not man's. The notion of love completely undercuts Stoic tranquility because love cannot be rationally calculated, measured, and controlled.

The tradition fails because its moral vision substituted duty for love, or, put another way, its humanity was only rational and therefore incomplete rather than fully human and therefore rational and complete. One must be careful not to make a simple pietistic judgment here. The tradition aimed high, but it was doomed in Faulkner's sense of the word: its inner nature generated an outward manifestation which in turn destroyed it; sooner or later it had to reap the consequence of the deficiency of its moral vision.

When Quentin shows Henry killing Bon because of miscegenation, he gives dramatic embodiment to the tradition's moral deficiency. The deficiency was not slavery but, negatively, lack of love, or, positively, spiritual pride; slavery was merely the accidental, historical form in which the deficiency expressed itself. There were other forms of its expression: for example, the social order which made the landless whites into objects—things—not free, responsible, deciding persons, but

cattle, creatures heavy and without grace, brutely evacuated into a world without hope or purpose for them, who would in turn spawn with brutish and vicious prolixity, populate, double treble and compound, fill space and earth with a race whose future would be a succession of cut-down and patched and made-over garments bought on exorbitant credit because they were white people, from stores where niggers were given the garments free. (235)

Quentin reports this as his grandfather's surmise of Sutpen's discovery as he tried to think through what to do about the affront at the plantation door. The deficiency also expressed itself in the military organization:

> battles lost not alone because of superior numbers and failing ammunition and stores, but because of generals who should not have been generals, who were generals not through training in contemporary methods or aptitude for learning them, but by the divine right to say 'Go there' conferred upon them by an absolute caste system; or because the generals of it . . . on one night and with a handful of men would gallantly set fire to and destroy a million dollar garrison of enemy supplies and on the next night be discovered by a neighbor in bed with his wife and be shot to death. (345-46)

Wash Jones's story is another case in point. Jones placed ultimate confidence in Sutpen's moral character: "Because you are brave," he says to Sutpen. "And I know that whatever your hands tech, whether hit's a regiment of men or a ignorant gal or just a hound dog, that you will make hit right" (284). Sutpen's inhuman pragmatism at last becomes clear to him when he hears Sutpen dealing with his granddaughter as if she were less a person even than his animal: "Well, Milly; too bad you're not a mare too. Then I could give you a decent stall in the stable" (286). At that moment, Wash too finds reality incredible and like Ellen succumbs to the shock of reality entering his life. *"I kaint have heard what I know I heard. I just know I kaint"* (288). And later: *"Better if his kind and mine too had never drawn the breath of life on this earth. Better that all who remain of us be*

*blasted from the face of it than that another Wash Jones
should see his whole life shredded from him and shrivel
away like a dried shuck thrown onto the fire"* (290-91).
Wash feels "no earth, no stability" (288) in a land where
such men "set the order and the rule of living . . . [and]
for the first time in his life he began to comprehend how it
had been possible for Yankees or any other army to have
whipped them" (290).

Such a society is doomed from within. In Rosa's sense, the
South was "a land primed for fatality and already cursed
with it" (21) not only because in the nature of things there
is that principle by which love must destroy what is against
it, but also because of the fate within evil itself. That the
evil results from a deficiency rather than from sin is a Stoic
and not a Christian judgment. "Deficiency" for the Christian is too weak a word. It is not a defect or a lack that is
responsible for evil, not a weakness of man's nature, but man
himself, all of himself. Quentin is correct in seeing that Sutpen and the tradition judge each other. But Faulkner sees
that the tradition failed itself, its own aims and virtues, because it wrongly assessed the nature of man, seeing only
defect where there was actually sin. From within the Stoic
tradition, it is correct to say that the curse of slavery destroys
the society. (To the true Stoic, of course, slavery was always
somewhat embarrassing, for it contradicts the Stoic doctrine
of the divine spark.) From without the Stoic tradition, however—that is, from the Christian point of view—the judgment that slavery destroys the society is superficial. Man
destroys the society because of his sin. Specifically, the sin
emerges historically and concretely as slavery.

Absalom, Absalom! shows that Allen Tate is both wrong
and right when he says that "it was not that slavery was
corrupt 'morally.' Societies can bear an amazing amount of
corruption and still produce high cultures. Black slavery

could not nurture the white man in his own image."[9] Tate points, in this fashion, to the historical and social means by which the society's destruction was accomplished. In another place, he makes it more explicit: "the Negro slave was a barrier between the ruling class and the soil" (272). Faulkner goes beyond Tate to show an intimate connection between the moral corruption and the alienation of the ruling class from the source of its values. In Reinhold Niebuhr's terms, a deep irony arising from a Christian realism is involved, a strength becoming weakness because of vanity prompted by the strength, virtue becoming vice "through some hidden defect in the virtue," catastrophe arising from "an unconscious weakness rather than . . . a conscious resolution."[10] Quentin's account, taken from his grandfather, provides ample evidence of how the white man is cut off from the source of his values.

When we turn to the way in which love accomplishes the destruction of what is against it in Sutpen's history, as compared with the tradition's, we find the same forces at work but against a lack of humanity in a distinctly modern sense. The tradition's human failure is, in a way, more easily dealt with in Christian terms because the Stoic society at least recognized that life is not unambiguously good, while Sutpen is "innocent" of the distinction between good and evil.

In the persons of Judith, Henry, and Bon, love works in a positive way to destroy Sutpen's design. Their love for each other only partially yields to his attempt to calculate, measure, and manipulate it because each of them finally forgives. A good case for calling Judith's action a renunciation and an expiation of her father's design is made by Cleanth Brooks, who sees the crucial difference between Judith and her father to lie in the fact that Judith is a woman who has

[9] *On the Limits of Poetry*, p. 274. (*Collected Essays*, p. 274.)
[10] *The Irony of American History*, p. viii.

a capacity to love. No wonder, then, that Mr. Compson can
explain her only by reference to a "true pride which can say
to itself without abasement *I love, I will accept no substitute;
something has happened between him and my father; if my
father was right, I will never see him again, if wrong he will
come or send for me; if happy I can be I will, if suffer I must
I can*" (*AA*, 121). Brooks goes on to point out that after
Bon's death, and Sutpen's, it is Judith who makes "the
acknowledgment of blood kinship" with Bon and his
descendants. Thereby "Sutpen's 'design' is repudiated; the
boy, even though he has the 'taint' of Negro blood, is not
turned away from the door."[11]

Mr. Compson observes that Henry's love for Judith when
compounded with his traditional upbringing puts him in a
situation where he must make a tragic choice between sister
and brother. "He felt, and acted immediately. He knew
loyalty and acted it, he knew pride and jealousy; he loved
grieved and killed, still grieving and, I believe, still loving
Bon" (*AA*, 96-97). Of course, Mr. Compson says this in
ignorance of Henry's real motive, but his words remain true
to the spirit of Quentin's recreation of Henry's tragedy. Sutpen had correctly calculated Henry's traditional response,
but even he knew that the playing of his "last trump card"
(274) would destroy his design and mean that he would
have to begin a third time. Henry's choice was tragic, I
should add, only within the situation as he perceived it.
Henry did not rise above the tradition as did Judith, but
Clytie claims forty-five years later that "whatever he done,
me and Judith and him have paid it out" (370).

Quentin and Shreve see Bon as sharing something of his
father's calculating, positivist spirit, for Bon manipulates
Henry and Judith to force Sutpen's recognition. His need in
this instance is essentially the one Sutpen experienced as a
child—to be treated as a person and not a thing—and he

11 "*Absalom, Absalom:* The Definition of Innocence," 552.

tries, like his father, to fulfill it by treating others as he has
been treated. Yet Quentin and Shreve also make a clear case
for Bon's capacity to love. They "correct" Mr. Compson's
version of the withdrawal to Pittsburgh Landing at the battle
of Shiloh. It is Bon who rescues the wounded Henry. And
when Henry comes to Bon after his interview with Sutpen,
in Carolina in 1865, Bon's first act, a fully compassionate
one, is to put his cloak about Henry's shoulders. But the
greatest act of love is in the matter of the octoroon's photograph found by Judith on Bon's body:

> And your old man wouldn't know about that too: why the black
> son of a bitch should have taken her picture out and put the
> octoroon's picture in, so he invented a reason for it. But I know.
> And you know too. Dont you? Dont you, huh? . . . It was because
> he said to himself, 'If Henry dont mean what he said, it will be all
> right; I can take it out and destroy it. But if he does mean what he
> said, it will be the only way I will have to say to her, *I was no
> good; do not grieve for me.*' Aint that right? Aint it? By God,
> aint it? (358-59)

In a negative way, love also works to destroy Sutpen's
design. Because he lacks the full humanity with which love
could endow him, his own calculating efforts are in vain.
Quentin and Shreve believe that one simple act of recognition from Sutpen toward Bon would have saved his whole
design:

> —*And he sent me no word? He did not ask you to send me to
> him? No word to me, no word at all? That was all he had to do,
> now, today; four years ago or at any time during the four years.
> That was all. He would not have needed to ask it, require it, of
> me. I would have offered it. I would have said, I will never see her
> again before he could have asked it of me. He did not have to do
> this, Henry. He didn't need to tell you I am a nigger to stop me.
> He could have stopped me without that, Henry.* (356)

And Sutpen himself is finally cut down when Jones attempts

to teach him what he was incapable of learning even from Time itself. Quentin thinks at first that the *"clock and calendar"* (181) must have taught him at last, but then visualizes eternity with Sutpen asking Jones, *"What was it, Wash? Something happened. What was it?"* (186). Love cannot force salvation.

VI

When Quentin settles upon the blood conflict between races as the key to Sutpen's failure, he also isolates the historical and formal element in the tradition which leads to its destruction. The novel gives us no reason to think that he has seen clearly into the heart of the tradition's vision of reality, the vision which generated its formal embodiments in social behavior and organization, or even that he understands fully the implications of Sutpen's innocence. But it does show his violent response to the failures of both traditional and modern men. One can compare his reaction with a reader's response to a poetic image. The power of the image does not depend upon the reader's cognitive understanding of the idea the image enacts. Nor does the creator of a powerful image need intellectual control of the idea. At the beginning of Chapter VI, we learn that all of *Absalom, Absalom!* is Quentin's answer to the demand that he *"tell about the South. What's it like there. What do they do there. Why do they live there. Why do they live at all"* (174). Quentin answers with the image of Sutpen and becomes caught up in his own image-making. In other words, Quentin evaluates the failures of traditional and modern men emotionally rather than intellectually. "Nevermore of peace" is the despairing summary of his search.

In the meantime, however, he has provided evidence both in the tale he tells and in the telling of it which is evaluated by Faulkner's aesthetic organization. It has been my thesis that the final view of reality emerging from the novel is not simply Quentin's or Sutpen's or the tradition's, but that it is the larger reality in the context of which the other realities emerge as dramatically credible. The context of the backstage action, I have said, is Quentin. But the final reality is the Christian one posited by a reading of the novel as a whole work of art, and it can be taken to be, if not Faulkner's own, at least the one to which he has in this novel given the broadest aesthetic embodiment and in terms of which he has made his most general judgment.

Absalom, Absalom! marks a shift in Faulkner's theological and fictive strategies. In *The Sound and the Fury* the Christian vision is juxtaposed with a modern one. Dilsey and Benjy stand over against Jason and Quentin. The tradition is treated only indirectly—as it emerges, that is, in Quentin's effete intellect—and the Christian vision is given embodiment in a fully developed character. Faulkner does not choose between his two main themes. In *Absalom, Absalom!* Faulkner goes behind Quentin, by going through him, to the tradition itself and also to the springs of the modern sensibility. He evaluates both not by embodying their Christian alternative in a main character but by setting them against each other in a Christian context which is wider than either.

In this novel, Faulkner is at once clearer about the content of the tradition, harder upon it, and less willing to sell it short by letting it be presented only in its decadent phase. He brings the Christian and Stoic alternatives together, tips the theological balance in favor of the Christian, but does not break their essential tension. The novel represents a movement but not a basic change within his theological center. The movement is subtle, though not as cautious as in "The Bear." The novel ends with an image of the despairing Quentin, still a "commonwealth" racked with disease and

lying impotent in the grip of an inherited evil which over-
whelms him. But Faulkner's Christian critique of the modern and traditional visions owes much to the Stoic. The
tradition is judged but not rejected; its human virtues are
still virtues but are to be attained in love rather than in
spiritual pride. An essentially different spirit than the Stoic
one is necessary even to attain the Stoic virtues. The novel
shows Faulkner still engaged in the theological enterprise
of defining the nature of reality by an aesthetic testing of
the facts of experience.

Morality with Passion:
A Study of "The Bear"

I

"THE BEAR" is theologically the most subtle work of the Faulkner corpus, and yet it is often taken to be the most simple. In *The Sound and the Fury* Faulkner juxtaposed themes without choosing between them, and in *Absalom, Absalom!* his choice, or at least the novel's final judgment, could be discerned only after a careful weighing of the whole book's aesthetic evidence. In "The Bear," however, Faulkner appears to have made his choice at last by giving us a hero unabashedly Christian, even Christlike.

The narrative method of "The Bear," though essentially the same as in the other stories we have examined, also seems to be less complex, that is, to employ simpler storytelling devices. Except for Part IV, we find a fairly straightaway hunting story which for the most part gives in chronological order the events in Isaac McCaslin's life to his eighteenth year. Even the fourth part, which comprehends almost all of Isaac's eighty-year life span (1867-1947), though certainly exhibiting a complex narrative structure within itself, appears only to complement or to make explicit in other terms the central meaning of the hunt narrative.

On this view, the most demanding task in interpretation of the work is to identify the reciprocal effects of the pagan, ritualistic, mythic motif in the hunt narrative (Parts I, II, III, and V) on the one hand and the Christian motif in the commissary conversation (Part IV) on the other. Faulkner obviously intends the hunt narrative to be read on more than one level. By the pitch of his rhetoric and sometimes by direct statement, we are told that the bear is immortally The Bear, that the feelings of the characters are primordial, that the wilderness is primeval, and that Sam Fathers is not merely a Negro and an Indian but that he is primal Man. The hunt narrative, in short, is allegory. As for Part IV, Isaac explains his relinquishment of the land (he will not accept the word "repudiation") by what he takes to be a Christian view of history, and he supports his view by reference to the events and meanings of the hunt narrative and to his discoveries while hunting through the plantation's commissary records. In other words, Part IV also makes claims beyond the limits of the story itself. It both comments upon and extends the allegory of the hunt narrative. If one takes Isaac's explanation at face value (he claims he is not trying to justify, merely to explain), his act of relinquishment is simply a formal and inevitable outcome of what is implied in the allegory. Certainly this is the way Isaac himself interprets his action in Part IV. A successful reading of "The Bear," then, must deal at least with its internal claim to be read as allegory. We shall discover, however, that this cannot suffice; not only is the allegory somewhat strained, but the fourth part serves to undercut it rather than to support it.

Internal to the story also is the demand that another basic reading of the hunt narrative be made. This second reading corrects Isaac's too facile, too romantic joining of his wilderness and commissary experiences. The second reading is both explicit and implicit, explicit in Cass's argument with Isaac and in the narrator's intrusion into the story, and implicit in the story's narrative method. The theological subtlety of "The Bear" lies in the narrative strategy whereby the meaning of the hunt narrative is progressively revised and the protagonist's apparently Christian vision is not allowed to stand. Faulkner does not wholly reject Isaac's theological interpretation of his experience, but he does show it to be limited from a Christian point of view and therefore inadequate from a human one.

As in most Faulkner narratives, point of view must be taken into account. But of special importance here, as in *Absalom, Absalom!,* is time of narration. Throughout, the moral, emotional, and intellectual distance of the narrator varies with his temporal stance. The first two parts and some of the third are given as if the present tense were on the morning of the day Old Ben is killed. The opening paragraph begins with "There was a man and a dog too *this* time"; the second paragraph begins with "He was sixteen. For six years *now* he had been a man's hunter. For six years *now* he had heard the best of all talking," and ends with "Thus it seemed to him *on this December morning.* . . ." The beginning of the third paragraph, however, enlarges the perspective; "He realised *later* that it had begun long *before* that" (*GDM,* 191-92, italics mine); and the narrator then ranges back in time to concentrate upon Isaac's tenth year, to bring him up to the present, the *now,* in Part III, and to proceed from there to the day's hunt.

The range of Part IV is even wider. In it, the narrator spreads before the reader a specious present. The foreground action is an evening conversation, in October of Isaac's twenty-first year, between Isaac and his cousin Cass Edmonds; but the narrative moves into the future as far as Isaac's last years and reaches into the past to the third generation. Since Part V concentrates on Isaac's visit to the scene of the hunt during his eighteenth year, Part IV radically interrupts the relatively normal chronology of the hunt narrative, but in such a way as to support its character as myth. In the specious present of Part IV where time is abolished, events already foregone, cause and effect (respectively, the wilderness-

commissary experience and the relinquishment of the land)
coeval, the events take on the unreality of a dream but the
certainty of preordination. The celebrated sentence of more
than sixteen hundred words, the two-page parenthesis, the
long sequence of paragraphs beginning with lower case letters, the twenty-page interruption of Isaac and Cass's conversation, the use of single inverted commas to indicate
dialogue, and the fragmentary, *non sequitur* character of
the dialogue itself—all of these devices, along with the narration's wide range, support the mythic quality of the hunt
narrative by abrogating the narrow impingement of time
and space upon the events and allowing them to partake of
the same mysterious quality of Isaac's own experience which
is described at one point as "shadowy in the limbo from
which time emerged and became time" (204).

Our first reading, the allegorical one, will be Isaac's.

II

The story of Isaac's experience in the wilderness
incorporates ritualistic patterns and primitive images familiar
to any cultural anthropologist, but more important it implies
myth. In his sixteenth year he participates in a hunting party
that kills a bear, Old Ben, in the wilderness north of Jefferson, and he discovers his family's secret sin of adultery and
incest committed by Carothers McCaslin, his grandfather
and the founder of his Mississippi heritage. These two events
constitute the pivotal point in his life because they provide
for him, for the most part in the order given, a vision of
good and evil. It is important that the first event occurs in
the wilderness while the second occurs in the commissary,
the "solar plexus" of the "tamed land," for in this way they
embrace the entire content of his life and occur in the context of his full heritage. Together the events reveal both

the human condition and the solution to it. Having lost his freedom by his sin, man now suffers alienation from the natural and psychic resources inherent in God's creation which can restore him to freedom if he will appropriate them with his heart. A solution to the alienation comes only with "the heart's truth," for only the heart can give a correct reading of God's purpose as it is contained in his Book (his Book is the created order as well as the Bible). What God has to say is too simple to be read except in love or in "the complexity of passion" (260). Isaac's wilderness experience, as well as what is to his mind the correlative experience in the commissary, discloses a truth, then, which he believes to be not simply personal but universal; it allows a vision of reality's fundamental moral character; and it provides for him an understanding of his and any man's relationship to the events of life in time and history.

The story itself, in other words, emerges as rite, as the initiation into a brotherhood of the chosen of God, which brotherhood infers the myth of moral manhood and, perhaps, a myth of human freedom. From the age of ten Isaac had gone with the hunting party to the big woods "to keep yearly rendezvous" with Old Ben, "the bear which they did not even intend to kill" (194). Even before he was allowed to accompany the party, for him Ben was not simply a bear or even *the* bear, "not even a mortal beast," but a mysterious symbol, "an anachronism indomitable and invincible out of an old dead time, a phantom, epitome and apotheosis of the old wild life . . . old Priam reft of his old wife and outlived all his sons" (193-94). It was Ben the phantom spirit of the virgin wilderness who "loomed and towered in his dreams," who "ran in his knowledge before he ever saw it" (193), whom they did not intend to kill, could not kill, and knew would not die; Old Ben, who when dead was still alive and free with "no heart to be driven and outraged, no flesh to be mauled and bled" (329). But it was Ben the bear, whose long history—to Isaac, a "legend"—"of corn-cribs broken down and rifled, of shoats and grown pigs and even calves carried bodily into the woods and devoured" (193) made him fair game, which they did pursue, try to kill, and did kill. Isaac learns suddenly that Ben is both of these things when Sam shows him the footprint; he is the bear of his memory and dreams but also a mortal bear whom they did not intend to kill because they had no hope of being cunning enough to do so.

When, with Sam Fathers beside him, he began "his novitiate to the true wilderness" at the age of ten, Isaac felt that "he was witnessing his own birth" (195). General Compson says that Isaac "was born knowing" what the "Sartorises and Edmondses invented farms and banks to keep . . . from having to find out" (250), namely the moral content of manhood, the wilderness virtues, the primary values of the ceremonially clean hunter: humility, pride, pity, patience, courage, and endurance. Although Isaac may have known these things when he was born, he cannot realize them until he is born again at "the yearly pageant-rite of the old bear's furious immortality" (194). He enters the wilderness as if entering a womb to be re-formed: in the wagon he sat "wrapped in the damp, warm, negro-rank quilt while the wilderness closed behind his entrance as it had opened momentarily to accept him, opening before his advancement as it closed behind his progress, no fixed path the wagon followed but a channel . . . the wagon progressing not by its own volition but by attrition of their intact yet fluid circumambience, drowsing, earless, almost lightless" (195). His new age, now that he is a new man, is dated at his rebirth: "He was only ten, only one week" (196). He is confirmed—the initiation is complete—in his sixteenth year. Only then is he prepared to learn the moral content of his plantation heritage, and indeed in the same month Ben is killed he takes down the commissary records to discover their secret.

In the figure of Sam Fathers the allegory of the hunt is collapsed. As a hunter he is implicated in Ben's death and as a Negro he is a reminder of old Carothers' guilt; he thus incarnates all that gives rise to Isaac's realization of his own personal-historical condition. His mere presence in the story is a reminder of its allegorical meaning: his taintless blood and life of wilderness virtue stand in judgment of the Mc-Caslin sin. Finally, in his life as a hunter close to the wilderness (his hut is within a half-mile of the hunting lodge), living in harmony with its rules, he exemplifies for Isaac the solution to the human condition. Isaac believes that Sam seeks his own death with foreknowledge and deliberation as he searches for the dog who can bay Ben. When he found him, *"he was glad. . . . He was old. He had no children, no people, none of his blood anywhere above earth that he would ever meet again. And even if he were to, he could not have touched it, spoken to it, because for seventy years now he had had to be a negro. It was almost over now and he was glad"* (215). When Ben comes near, Sam's nostrils arch, his face becomes alive. When he speaks of Ben he calls him "the head bear," "the man" (198), as his own father was called "The Man" or *L'homme* or Doom. At the age of thirteen Isaac tells him that when Ben is killed "it must be one of us. So it wont be until the last day. When even he dont want it to last any longer" (212). When Boon, who is also "one of us," kills Ben, Sam "quits," literally lies down and dies (it is probable that Boon killed Sam at Sam's request), feeling released to "go home" (245). He dies with a "profound look" (245), speaking his Indian tongue, and "only the boy knew that Sam too was going to die" (246). Isaac feels these incidents to be a pattern of birth and death lying in the very nature of things, exhibited also in the

seasons' "ordered immortal sequence, the deathless and im-
memorial phases of the mother who had shaped him if any
had toward the man he almost was" (326).

The figure of Lion, a leading protagonist of the hunt, is
ambiguous. On the one hand he is the cold, impersonal
killing machine of civilization who dooms Ben, the spirit
of the wilderness, just as the machines (axes and logging
trains and sawmills) doom the wilderness. On the other hand
he is a dog of stature, big as Ben is big, as the woods are big,
as Isaac's rifle is too big, and as Boon is big and childish. He
is a dog equal in his own right to Ben who is "the head bear."
In this way the figure of Lion catches up the power of two
of the allegorical protagonists, the wilderness and the new
culture. Only when Lion joins the hunt do the swampers
and townspeople come into the hunting camp in real expec-
tation of seeing Ben subdued, and their presence shows this
to be an affair of a wider community than just the hunting
party. When Isaac and Sam fail to shoot at Ben after Isaac's
fyce has caused Ben to bay within easy range, they rationalize that it was not right yet. The situation in which Ben
would die had to be one befitting the stature of his life.
It could not be a routine hunt; there had to be a Lion.
When Lion does appear, Isaac feels the "stage" is set for
its last act (226); also, by that time, Isaac had been ceremonially cleansed by the blood of his first deer ("The Old
People," 164). Lion, trailing Ben, gives no exultant cry,
and the yapping of the other dogs underscores his deliberate
single-mindedness. When Ben bays, he catches Lion in "both
arms, almost loverlike" (240), while Lion presses in without
slackening, just as the buzz saw of civilization's lumbering
camps plows into the knotty wood with a seeming burst of
speed and power. As Ben "dont care no more for bears than
he does for dogs or men neither" (198), so Lion "cared
about no man and no thing" (220).

In seeking his own death, Sam captured and trained Lion.
But Boon took over his feeding, care, and companionship.

The figure of Boon possesses the same ambiguity as Lion. He is a mongrel but tainted, while Sam and Lion are taintless. One of his virtues (or vices, says Cass) is absolute fidelity to Major de Spain and Cass. Yet though faithful, he is unreliable; though brave, he is, like Isaac's fyce, improvident. Isaac, sensitive to his simpleminded humanity ("he had the mind of a child, the heart of a horse" [227]), gives him a dollar for a drink of whiskey when he recalls Boon's gentle toughness with a spotted horse. And Boon, sensitive to his own failure before Lion to hit—after five shots!—the old bear at bay, says, "I aint fit to sleep with him" (226). However, for all this, Boon is a machine as Lion is a machine. His face looks like a walnut carved with a machinist's hammer, and his "shoe-button eyes" are "without depth or meanness or generosity or viciousness or gentleness or anything else" (227). The stubble on his face is "blue . . . like the filings from a new gun-barrel" (231). And in the last scene of the story he catches up the values of the machine civilization, telling Isaac to keep away from the tree full of frantic squirrels: "They're mine!" Just so, Lion is a machine with "cold yellow eyes . . . [and with a body of a] strange color like a blued gun-barrel" (218). The yellow eyes are "not fierce and there was nothing of petty malevolence in them, but a cold and almost impersonal malignance like some natural force" (218).

While Sam and Ben personify the wilderness and the old culture, Boon and Lion appear to be *bridges* to the new and encroaching culture. Consequently, it was right, Isaac believed as a man, that Boon and not Sam should be identified with Lion. Sam had too much of Old Ben in him. It was right that Boon, "his huntsman," "should have nursed the dogs," and killed the bear, for Sam was "the chief, the prince" (222), not possessive of the dog (as Boon was possessive of the dog and the squirrels), caring only for the significance of the hunt. Boon, "the plebeian," could see only the kill, the hunt, and like a machine he killed without sensitivity to the old culture he was killing. With his knife, a personal weapon, a city weapon, he found the wilderness's heart, and as Cass implied when he asked "Did you kill him, Boon?" (253), he had also found the heart of his old chief. But it was Boon the sensitive child and serf, who would fight to deny his Indian blood when sober and to affirm it when drunk, who stood on the grave of Lion to challenge Cass and to fulfill the wishes of his prince, his chief.

In the same month of December, 1883, in which Old Ben was killed, Isaac discovered in the plantation records that in June, 1833, Tomasina, the Negro slave and daughter of old Carothers McCaslin by his slave Eunice, died while giving birth to Carothers' child. Eunice had committed suicide six months earlier. To Isaac as a child the old records in the commissary had appeared harmless though formidable. But at sixteen when he took them down "he knew what he was going to find before he found it" (268). Isaac felt he had discovered the particular form in which violation of the wilderness virtues expressed itself in his personal heritage. He was prepared for this discovery because of his moral education in the wilderness.

From Isaac's point of view, then, his relinquishment of the land at the age of twenty-one is the active expression of what was latent in his wilderness experience. There he had learned from Sam that violation of the land, the wilderness too, derived from the root sin of spiritual pride. The white man's sin (the Indian was also guilty of it) is the old, the Original, sin of pride made manifest in his desire to possess the land and the Negro; it is the same sin as in the Old Testament story of the fall: of power without sensitivity, of knowledge without love. The history of the tension between the wilderness and the tamed land reveals a moral order in which sin works its own punishment.

Part IV shows Isaac generalizing from his own condition in order to explain his decision of relinquishment. In doing so he falls back upon a theological argument in the form of an interpretation of history. All is said in the context of his personal experience, but his personal experience is widened to include a sensitivity to his American and especially his southern heritage.

He believes his decision is commensurate with God's purpose in history, which is to set man free, free of the consequences of his prehistorical fall. Isaac develops his argument in the highly charged language of nineteenth-century southern rhetoric. Out of "the old world's worthless twilight" (258) came the American possibility. God had "used a simple egg to discover to them a new world where a nation of people could be founded in humility and pity and sufferance and pride of one to another" (258). The history of mankind is the history of the refusal or failure of man to accept the gift of redemption. With patience, but without hope, God offered the possibility again to America. He created the McCaslins of this world, thinks Isaac, to destroy the evil which the McCaslins of this world had brought into it.

Isaac believes America's sin to have arisen out of a conviction of its own innocence; because they were in a new world the early Americans thought themselves new men. His mention of the American dream shows he is aware of the kind of nineteenth-century humanistic optimism which made Lyman Beecher exclaim that "if it had been the design of heaven to establish a powerful nation, in the full enjoyment of civil and religious liberty, where all the energies of man might find scope and excitement, on purpose to show the world by experiment, of what man is capable; . . . where could such an experiment have been made but in this country. . . ."[1] In this period of American nationalism even "wise men hoped,"[2] said Whitehead; and Melville, from

[1] *The Memory of our Fathers, A Sermon Delivered at Plymouth, on the Twenty-Second of December, 1827* (Boston: T. R. Marvin, 1828), p. 17.

[2] Alfred North Whitehead, "The Study of the Past—its Uses and its

whose *Moby Dick* many of the images in Faulkner's story
are taken, could believe that the new world was literally
Heaven, not a Paradise now, "but to be made so at God's
good pleasure. . . . The seed is sown, and the harvest must
come; and our childrens' children, on the world's jubilee
morning, shall all go with their sickles to the reaping. Then
shall the curse of Babel be revoked, a new Pentecost come,
and the language they shall speak shall be the language of
Britain."[3]

The South's particular sin is slavery, but Isaac believes
the South to be dear to God in a way the North is not. The
North, too, expressed spiritual pride in its own form of
possessiveness. Rugged individualism of the new industrial-
ism expressing itself economically in *laissez-faire* capitalism
produced a spiritual arrogance which could not go unpun-
ished. God's purpose was lost in the celebration of the
boundlessness of the human spirit, while with ruthless
rapacity and greed the North manufactured for a profit the
products of the southern society it condemned. At least,
Isaac feels, the southerner had some human compassion for
his slaves, but that was not enough. The Civil War was the
price paid by the entire nation. God's mercy may be endless
but his patience is not: *"This is enough,"* and looking about
for one more time "upon this land this South for which He
had done so much" (283), and upon the East and West and
North "passing resolutions about horror and outrage in
warm and air-proof halls" (284), God saw that *"Apparently
they can learn nothing save through suffering, remember
nothing save when underlined in blood"* (286). The Civil

Dangers," *Essays in Science and Philosophy* (New York: Philosophical
Library, 1948), p. 114.
   [3] Herman Melville, *Redburn, His First Voyage, Being the Sailor-boy Con-
fessions and Reminiscences of the Son of a Gentleman in the Merchant
Service,* Standard ed. (London: Constable and Co., Ltd., 1922), Ch. xxxiii,
p. 217.

War, however, failed to teach the nation: *"Apparently there is a wisdom beyond even that learned through suffering necessary for a man to distinguish between liberty and license"* (289-90). The Reconstruction, "that dark corrupt and bloody time" (289), followed, and the "third race," the carpetbaggers, with "a single fierce will for rapine and pillage" (290), continued to thwart God's purpose to set man free. (The narrator, speaking from Isaac's point of view, identifies the KKK as a foreign, carpetbag element.)

The wisdom beyond that learned through suffering is the wisdom of freedom. It is what Isaac feels he has learned from his wilderness experience, especially from Sam who as a Negro "had learned humility through suffering and learned pride through the endurance which survived the suffering" and as an Indian could learn from Ben "the fierce pride of liberty and freedom" (295). Paradoxically, the Negro and the land, the objects of man's spiritual pride, have become the agents of God's purpose to deliver man from the consequences of his pride and grant him freedom. Isaac implies that the Negro is really without taint; all of his vices are simply aped from the white man and his virtues are his own. Thus "Sam Fathers set me free" (300) is Isaac's final declaration that he is himself one chosen to carry out God's purpose.

Within a decade after the animus (machine) of civilization conquered the wilderness, Isaac relinquishes his claim to the land as something he can own according to man's laws. But he does not repudiate the land, for it is the agent of deliverance; he inherits it in spirit from his spiritual father. It was Sam's land to bequeath because he had used it properly and it is now Isaac's to receive because he is, through Sam, identified with the community of God's chosen who "hold the earth mutual and intact in the communal anonymity of brotherhood" (257).

Isaac was, in the wilderness rite, initiated into the brotherhood of the chosen—chosen, of course, in the sense that the Jews were chosen: through suffering to bear witness to God's purpose. Sam had freed him of the legalistic, rationalistic, calculating spirit of civilization. Just as he had had to divest himself of his watch, his compass, and his gun in order to experience the vision of the spirit of the wilderness, so, after his experience was completed in the final hunt, he had to divest himself not only of the legal holding of the land but also of his more recent heritage from his father, Uncle Buck, of a countinghouse manumission of the Negro. Operating now with "the heart's truth," Isaac, appropriately, takes up the carpenter's tools, "because if the Nazarene had found carpentering good for the life and ends He had assumed and elected to serve, it would be all right too for Isaac McCaslin" (309).

III

In Part IV, then, Isaac feels he has acted upon the allegorical meaning of the other parts. He has read his total experience—in the wilderness and in the commissary—as a unified and coherent one clearly dictating his personal role and response. But Isaac's reading is not the only one offered in "The Bear." A second reading, incipient in the hunt narrative itself, becomes predominant in Part IV and governs the reader's response to Part V. This second reading is provided by the story's fictive strategy taken in its totality; that is, Isaac's reading is qualified by Cass's interpretation of Isaac's experience and by the narrator's fuller, less sympathetic and less romantic presentation of Isaac's interior life both in the foreground action and in his later experiences.

Cass does not interpret Isaac's experience from the position of a passive observer making judgments on the basis of apparent facts. He is Isaac's "father almost" (297, 308), so deeply involved in his development that Sam Fathers, who also had two fathers, "always referred to the boy's cousin as his father, establishing . . . that relation between them . . . of the child to the man who sired his flesh and his thinking too" ("The Old People," 174). Cass first brought Isaac to the big woods, gave him the breech-loader with the silver inlaid trigger guard (205), gave him the compass by which he hunted (199), the same compass he had to relinquish in abrogation of the ancient rules of hunting in order to have his first vision of Old Ben. Later, it is from Cass that he borrows the thirty dollars to buy new carpenter tools. Cass shares with Isaac the very core of his cultural experience. In "The Old People" he shows understanding of the growing process through which Isaac is going, confessing to Isaac that he too had experienced in Sam's company a mystical vision of a tall buck after he had killed his first deer (187). Thus it is fitting that it be to Cass that Isaac give his "explanation":

'Let me talk now. I'm trying to explain to the head of my family something which I have got to do which I dont quite understand myself, not in justification of it but to explain it if I can. I could say I dont know why I must do it but that I do know I have got to because I have got myself to have to live with for the rest of my life and all I want is peace to do it in.' (288)

Cass was the one to mold the very way Isaac thinks about his experience. In the course of the foreground conversation, both recall the time seven years earlier when Isaac had failed to shoot Old Ben at close range after the bear had been bayed by Isaac's fyce. At that time Cass had seen an analogy between Keats's paradoxical truth in "Ode on a Grecian Urn" and the truth Isaac had just experienced. By an *explication de texte* he tried to help Isaac understand and accept his refusal to shoot Old Ben. It was, as in Keats, a moment of Platonic Truth. It was an insight into reality in terms of the nature of becoming and being, of motion and stasis, of change and fixity, of time and eternity. The speaker in the poem had found the insight "frozen" on his urn. He had envied the bold lover his eternity, his fixity, his stasis, his being, because the lover had thereby escaped the need to grieve.

The evil of passage in time is more than the loss of immediacy with the consummation of the act, the loss of the value of the hunt, the pursuit, the chase; it is also the disappointment that comes with surfeit. In life, in becoming, one must necessarily move on, become something else, and must, being human, inevitably grieve. Had Isaac killed Old Ben he would have had to grieve, to accept the end, really, of himself. All after that act could only be disappointment. Cass was, as it turned out, right about Isaac's innate temperament, for at Ben's death not only did Sam "quit" and Boon Hogganbeck become an officer of the ensuing decay, but Isaac quit too. His whole life entered a period of stasis in the ideal and decline in the actual. Cass had read Isaac accurately. But the point is, it was Cass, as the sire of his thinking, who had first introduced him to the terms by which he could articulate himself and justify his vision and decision.

Cass had told Isaac that truth itself, like the bold lover and his maiden, is static. It is, as Plato and Keats said, the same as Beauty and, as Plato puts it, the same as Being itself. In *The Symposium* Diotima describes to Socrates the vision of beauty as a mystical, sudden experience of revelation. The initiate who has been properly prepared for a vision of beauty by "the mysteries of love, . . . will suddenly have revealed to him . . . a beauty whose nature is marvellous indeed, the final goal":

> This beauty is first of all eternal; it neither comes into being nor passes away, . . . he will see it as absolute, existing alone with itself, unique, eternal, and all other beautiful things as partaking of it, yet in such a manner that, while they come into being and

pass away, it neither undergoes any increase or diminution nor suffers any change.[4]

Isaac, the initiate, had been prepared for this revelation by the mystery rites of the wilderness. At the age of twelve, when he shot his first deer and Sam had marked him with the slain blood, Diotima's vision was made concrete for him in the frozen image of the buck's death:

> the buck still and forever leaped, the shaking gun-barrels coming constantly and forever steady at last, crashing, and still out of his instant of immortality the buck sprang, forever immortal. ("The Old People," 178)

Cass had also told Isaac that truth, as he had experienced it in the fyce incident, is not only eternal and unchanging: *"Truth is one. It doesn't change. It covers all things which touch the heart—honor and pride and pity and justice and courage and love"* (297). When, in the foreground conversation, Isaac explains his decision to Cass, he uses Cass's very words about truth. It is "the heart's truth" that he has found. But Cass does not accept the language this time. Perhaps he had reread the poem. It is almost as if he had read Cleanth Brooks's interpretation of the poem in the meantime. Brooks, who gives a standard reading, finds the poem's central paradox to lie in the phrase "Cold Pastoral," for the pastoral (a word connoting warmth) is of marble men and maidens. The insight of the frieze is of Reality, perhaps, and even of reality's tragic dimension, but certainly not of life. "The beauty portrayed is deathless because it is lifeless," says Brooks.[5] Isaac makes passion into a *thing*, preserves its form but voids its feeling, traps it in what Berg-

---

[4] *The Symposium*, trans. W. Hamilton (Baltimore: Penguin Books, Inc., 1951), pp. 93-94.

[5] Cleanth Brooks, "Keats's Sylvan Historian: History Without Footnotes," *The Well Wrought Urn: Studies in the Structure of Poetry* (New York: Harcourt, Brace, and Co., 1947), p. 144.

son would call "an eternity of death" which is "nothing else than the movement emptied of the mobility which made its life."[6] In his prefatory note to *The Mansion*, Faulkner himself says that " 'living' is motion, and 'motion' is change and alteration and therefore the only alternative to motion is un-motion, stasis, death." Isaac's vision is of the "alternative to motion" but without the death; his vision is a denial of life, an insight, really, only into unfeeling objects immune from time.

In effect, Cass refutes his own teachings, not only by argument but also by the simple gesture of indicating the commissary records. For *there* is truth in time, in history. The records are Isaac's patrimony as much as the land; that is, they show what the land means. Cass has thought back through the tragic truth to the reality from which it arises. There, from the reality of the historical experience, comes truth. The fading pages are to him "the frail and iron thread strong as truth and impervious as evil and longer than life itself and reaching beyond record and patrimony both to join him with the lusts and passions, the hopes and dreams and *griefs*" of all mankind (299, italics mine). For Isaac these same pages are "*frail* as truth," although they are "yet cable-strong to bind for life them who made the cotton to the land their sweat fell on" (256, 293-94, italics mine). But they bind only for "a little while yet" (294).

Cass has other arguments. Isaac cannot relinquish what he does not have; therefore, old Carothers had to own the land to bequeath it to Isaac to relinquish. Cass is saying that Isaac must *repudiate* if he relinquishes. This is more than a quibbling over terms, for Cass is holding that one must begin with existence as given, that one must act with reference to reality if he is to act effectively upon that reality.

---

[6] Henri Bergson, *An Introduction to Metaphysics*, trans. T. E. Hulme, 2nd ed., The Library of Liberal Arts, No. 10 (New York: The Liberal Arts Press, 1955), p. 47.

Further, Isaac admits that his act is an attempt to escape the doom of old Carothers' fatal blood. But Cass sees his repudiation as an escape therefore from responsibility. The way in which he is attempting to escape his doom is the way of "self-sufficient finitude"; he is compounding sin rather than expiating it, evading responsibility for the human condition rather than accepting it and suffering for it, denying the continuity of historical experience rather than recognizing and acting within it. Cass has completely abandoned the Platonic aversion to becoming and motion. He has accepted life and therefore change and motion and grief.

Faulkner's Cass, in other words, finds himself in the position of Sophocles' Creon of *Antigone* or Melville's Captain Vere of *Billy Budd*. "We never see the real meaning of 'original sin,' " says Emil Brunner, "we never perceive the depth and the universality of evil, or what evil really means in the depths common to us all, until we are *obliged* to do something which, in itself, is evil; that is, we do not see this clearly until we are obliged to do something in our official capacity—for the sake of order, and therefore for the sake of love—which, apart from our 'office,' would be absolutely wrong."[7] Isaac tries to remove himself from the position where he is obliged to act officially, but Cass, to whom the land falls with Isaac's relinquishment, accepts the responsibility and with it the obligation to act within the limits of his finitude. *He,* not Isaac, accepts the tragic character of the human condition in which man is, existentially, caught between the demands of Gospel and Law, in which one must live with the tension between love and justice. Cass has the courage of Henry Sutpen who "loved grieved and killed, still grieving and . . . still loving" (*AA,* 97).

Cass is also like Charles Mallison who believes that "life is not so much motion as an inventless repetition of motion"

[7] *A Study in Christian Ethics: The Divine Imperative,* trans. Olive Wyon (Philadelphia: The Westminster Press, 1947), p. 227.

(*M*, 197). Isaac therefore cannot avoid sharing the lusts and passions of others; he will, with all men, dream and hope, and he will have to grieve (Isaac's later history bears out Cass's insight). When Isaac declines the altar (*GDM*, 283), he exhibits the ultimate in spiritual pride—a failure to trust God, a desire, arising from the anxiety accompanying sin, to control the process of salvation himself. Isaac is providing his own escape, for "maybe this time the exasperated Hand might not supply the kid" (283).

So, Cass "did not even gesture" toward the records when Isaac declared, "I am free." "No, not now nor ever," Cass replied. "I am what I am; I will be always what I was born and have always been" (299-300). As for Isaac, will he, nill he, if he inherits the land from Sam Fathers he also inherits it from his grandfather. "All [are] Grandfather" (283), all are tainted and not free. Isaac too is only what he is.

IV

A further corrective of Isaac's reading is provided by the narrator's tone. We have already noted that the moral, emotional, and intellectual distance of the narrator varies with his temporal stance. This is true but it is not the whole story, for finally, I believe, one must say that the narrative point of view is inconsistent to the point of being so complex that it can become confusing. Probably O'Connor's study of the story's genesis explains the reason for this. O'Connor believes that the inconsistencies in Isaac's character reflect a general failure in *Go Down, Moses* to integrate the themes of injustice to the Negro and man's proper relationship to nature. He assigns a partial reason for the failure to Faulkner's unsuccessful attempt to merge two earlier stories, a shorter version of "The Bear" and a story entitled "Lion."[8]

But the difficulty does not lie in the hunt narrative so much as in the relationship of the hunt narrative to Part IV. The greatest point of inconsistency is not between Isaac of the hunt narrative and Isaac of the commissary conversation. Rather, it is in the narrative tone, the narrator's attitude toward his materials. Isaac may be inconsistent; that is to say, he may have misread his wilderness experience or he may be incapable of living up to the wilderness virtues in the context of civilization. But in that case—and it does appear to be the case—he is simply wrong or inadequate and his being wrong or inadequate becomes part of his character. There is no inherent demand in storytelling that a character show consistency, but there is a demand that the story as a whole be coherent. Nor does inconsistency even in narrative tone preclude coherence, but it can lead to a complexity which tends to confuse. In "The Bear" Faulkner borders on such a confusion. But in the story as a whole, he turns the complexity of narrative tone to good account, making it function finally as one more element within the story which qualifies the story's apparent allegory to the extent of undercutting it.

The complexity of narrative tone causes the reader to revise his judgments as he goes along. In the hunt narrative the narrator is, for the most part, sympathetic with Isaac and enlists the reader's approval of his romantic response to his experience. We are prepared from the opening paragraphs for a story that is "the best of all talking" (191), "the best of all breathing," and "the best of all listening,"

8 William Van O'Connor, "The Wilderness Theme," *The Tangled Fire of William Faulkner* (Minneapolis: University of Minnesota Press, 1954), pp. 125-34. The earliest version of "The Bear" can be found in *The Saturday Evening Post*, CCXIV (May 9, 1942), 30-31, 74, 76, 77. "Lion" appears in *Harper's Monthly Magazine*, CLXXII (December 1935), 67-77.

a story of "the best game of all" (192) pursued by men who are "not white nor black nor red but men, hunters, with the will and hardihood to endure and the humility and skill to survive" (191). We are prepared for a story of the plebeian and the noble, of the tainted and the taintless, of the corruptible and the incorruptible. We are, in other words, prepared for a fully romantic tale of a young boy's growth to manhood in the wilderness.

It soon becomes apparent that there is a symbolic tension in the romantic tale which threatens to destroy it. "So he should have hated and feared Lion," a phrase repeated three times in Part II (209, 212, 226), begins to reinforce the other evidences of tension which have become only vaguely apparent in the figures of Sam and Boon. By the last paragraph of Part II, the reader is told that the whole action of the story, in Isaac's mind, is caught up in a "fatality." "It was like the last act on a set stage" (226). The change of tone in Part IV is thus prepared for. The contrast between the wilderness and the tamed land and the tension between the wilderness virtues and the motif of injustice to the Negro have emerged in the hunt narrative itself. But in Part IV they *are* the story itself, for the focus of the narrative is cognitive rather than dramatic. Part IV is argumentative and intellectual, a story of ideas. The dramatic elements of Part IV function to support the ideas, while the idea content of the hunt narrative is for the most part not essential to the story. The hunt narrative, in other words, stands as story before it stands as allegory.

The shift in tone in Part IV makes the earlier sympathetic tone appear as ironic.[9] The reader, like Isaac, must look back

[9] This position is in general agreement with Herbert A. Perluck's " 'The Heart's Driving Complexity': An Unromantic Reading of Faulkner's 'The Bear,' " in *Accent*, XX (Winter 1960), 23-46. Perluck's thesis is that "The Bear" is not "a romantic Christian pastoral of redemption," but that "chiefly through ironic means" (23) Faulkner presents "a story of a renunciation that fails, as they all must. It is also the story of man's ineluctable

upon the hunt, but, unlike Isaac, he sees it in a new light. By the time Cass has had his say, by the time the tension between the wilderness virtues and Negro slavery has been pointed up and discussed at length, and by the time the private bedroom scene has assassinated the image of Isaac's public posture, the earlier story of the hunt has taken on a completely different feel.

What has made all the difference is the narrative tone of Part IV which openly admits an attitude toward Isaac obscured by the romantic tone of the earlier parts. When explaining to Cass his vision of God's plan for deliverance through a chosen people, Isaac pauses:

> 'They [Negroes] will outlast us because they are–' it was not a pause, barely a falter even, possibly appreciable only to himself, as if he couldn't speak even to McCaslin, even to explain his repudiation, that which to him too, even in the act of escaping (and maybe this was the reality and the truth of his need to escape) was heresy: so that even in escaping he was taking with him more of that evil and unregenerate old man who could summon, because she was his property, a human being because she was old enough and female, to his widower's house and get a child on her and then dismiss her because she was of an inferior race, and then bequeath a thousand dollars to the infant because he would be dead then and wouldn't have to pay it, than even he had feared. 'Yes. . . . They are better than we are. Stronger than we are.' (294)

In his explanation of the meaning of this faltering, the narrator enters into the debate between Isaac and Cass in such a way as to tip the balance in favor of Cass's position. He allows us to see that Isaac is not so fully divested of in-

---

fate of being only man. And on another level, it is a parable of man's pride, in his trying to be more than man, and of the evil this pride accomplishes in its condescending ascription of all that man does not want to see in himself to a certain few untouchables, the Boons of the world" (25). Perluck stresses that "the romantic 'meaning' is Ike's 'meaning'—the way he would prefer to view the events in which he has participated and his own motives—but it is not ultimately Faulkner's" (33).

herited evil as he likes to believe, and he shows that privately
Isaac thinks of his act as an escape through repudiation.

The shift in narrative tone is apparent in many other
instances. In the account of Isaac's search through the records
we learn that he cannot allow himself an unbuffered shock
from reality: between old Carothers and Tomasina *"there
must have been love* he thought. *Some sort of love . . . .
not just an afternoon's or a night's spittoon"* (270). We are
given by implication a desperation of tone in all of Isaac's
arguments, as if he were making his last stand. At the close
of the foreground conversation he is not even listening to
Cass's replies, but abstractly, dreamily telling himself that
"Sam Fathers set me free" (300). He stands impotent before Fonsiba's "narrow, thin, too thin coffee-colored face
watching him without alarm, without recognition, without
hope" and hears her assert, "I'm free" (280). When he
speaks the same phrase to Cass it takes on something of
the same emptiness because it is spoken as from a dream.
Carefully he insists that the thirty dollars for new tools is
a loan, but then accepts without protest the thirty-dollar
monthly deposit from his patrimony. The reader also
becomes aware of his sterility as "Uncle Ike," "uncle to
half a county and still father to none" (300), and finds
reason to believe that Isaac might very well have explained
his relinquishment by saying that "all I want is peace" (288).

Isaac never gives up his original and romantic perceptions,
his tendency to fix reality in a frieze as on the urn. Herbert
A. Perluck's "unromantic reading" of "The Bear" emphasizes
this aspect of Isaac's sensibility. He tries to live as if life
were a "poem," a play, unbound by time and space and logic.
For Isaac, "the final meanings are discovered in the *memory*
of action, of life, in poetry and in the heart."[10] Isaac's imagi-

10 Perluck, p. 34.

nation is perhaps best described as poetic or "literary" in the sense in which Faulkner has Charles Mallison use the term in *The Town:* the passions of life are fixed "in the most general and unspecific and impersonal terms of the literary and dramatic lay-figures of the protagonists of passion in their bloodless and griefless posturings of triumph or anguish" (305). In order to make the passions of life griefless, he must make them bloodless. He is no Quentin Compson, despairing that the flux of life will heal the anguish of its wounds. Isaac refuses to wound, lets Boon wield the knife, and *he* will heal the wound and avoid the grief by transporting Ben and Lion to some eternal specious present where they are still engaged in "the long challenge and the long chase, [the one with] no heart to be driven and outraged, [the other with] no flesh to be mauled and bled."[11]

Isaac appropriates for life the strategy of art. The superiority of art, as Brooks suggests in his analysis of Keats's "Ode on a Grecian Urn," is precisely that it, unlike life itself, does not allow human passion to become cloyed.[12] Cass had found a willing listener in the young Isaac when he pointed to the frozen beauty, the uncloyed passions on the urn, and for the rest of his life Isaac kept this perception of being and beauty as his reality. As Perluck says, he therefore "didn't *have* to grieve, because removing himself from life's commitment, he could view the approaching event [of Ben's death] in his play-acting Hamlet-like aesthetic perspective, as the 'last act on a set stage,' and thus obviate the necessity to *live* the shattering event."[13] Perluck sees that

what remains in the imagination long after one has puzzled

[11] Without the interpolations, this quotation is given as it appears on p. 329 of *Go Down, Moses.* The interpolations reconstruct the original phrasing in "Lion," *Harper's Monthly Magazine,* 77.

[12] Brooks, *The Well Wrought Urn,* p. 146.

[13] Perluck, p. 40.

through the difficult *argument* of "The Bear" is the fixed, frieze-like image of the hunt, in which the ennobling pursuit *and* the slaying, the "poem" *and* life, are inextricably suspended. Ike himself sees it in these terms. . . . The thwarted, wounded sense in Faulkner of the flow and passage of acts in time is thus manifested usually by images which are the opposite of movement but which convey in tragic tension the completeness of being, of art, and the incompleteness of becoming, of life. (36)

Since the reader comes to Part V armed with Part IV's irony, his initial response to the continuation of the hunt narrative is no longer the same. The narrator causes him to look ironically upon the figure of Isaac who stands before the immaculately dressed Major de Spain but sees him as he used to be, "in boots and muddy corduroy, unshaven, sitting the shaggy powerful long-hocked mare with the worn Winchester carbine across the saddlebow and the great blue dog standing motionless as bronze at the stirrup" (*GDM,* 317). And when Isaac escapes the rattler, the snake, "the old one, the ancient and accursed about the earth . . . walking on two feet" (329), escapes by a statue-like freezing of his motion, he now symbolically prefigures for the reader the method by which he will try to escape from the curse of his heritage. He will try to crystallize the flow of life and live in the unrealism of a private dream world where evil is avoided, although it is acknowledged with "Chief . . . Grandfather" (330).

Because of the glimpse into the static sensibility of Isaac in his later life given in Part IV, one tends to read Part V, where Isaac is eighteen years old, as if he is in fact the pathetic old man he is destined to be. Once a year for the next fifty years he will attempt "to hide himself . . . once more anyway" (318) from the evidences of civilization's encroachment upon the wilderness by returning to the big woods to hunt. In the closing scene of the story—Boon under the tree full of frantic squirrels and shouting "They're mine!"—the roles of Isaac and Boon could be reversed. Indeed, Boon too, in his own limited way, is showing sensitivity to the passing values embodied in the wilderness. His possessiveness, here so blatantly material, is the obverse of Isaac's spiritual possessiveness. In "inventless repetition" of the mistake of America's founding fathers, Isaac believes that the woods and the game in it are "truly" his because he is untainted and free, a new man in a new world.

The most significant single amendment of Isaac's reading is the bedroom scene which concludes Part IV. Its position in the story is strategic, coming as it does after Isaac's discovery of the family secret, after his affirmation of freedom in the argument with Cass, after descriptions of his abortive attempts to distribute the thousand-dollar legacies, and after the account of his own empty legacy from the female Beauchamp line, yet just before the return in his eighteenth year to the big woods. Isaac is about twenty-eight (the scene can be variously dated). The position of the incident allows it a double reference, to what Isaac believes to be the nature of his private role and to what Cass—and the narrative tone—holds to be the truth. The narrator has already warned the reader of what he will find: "1874 the boy; 1888 the man, repudiated denied and free; 1895 and husband but no father, unwidowered but without a wife, and found long since that no man is ever free and probably could not bear it if he were" (281).

In the bedroom incident Isaac's early vision of integrity is compromised. He succumbs to the patent sexuality of his for the first time visibly naked wife. There is the revelation that he did want a son, although in "Delta Autumn" we find that he had never intended through his progeny to involve himself in that pattern of inheriting, possessing, and bequeathing the wilderness had taught him to decline. Rather, in relinquishing the land he had hoped "at least [to] save and free his son" from the shame and wrong of the

McCaslin patrimony (351). But in the bedroom scene, the wilderness' "best of all talking" and listening and breathing is debased by association with the action of his wife: *"She already knows more than I with all the man-listening in camps where there was nothing to read ever even heard of. They are born already bored with what a boy approaches only at fourteen and fifteen with blundering and aghast trembling. . . . She is lost. She was born lost. We were all born lost"* (314). Supposedly his man-listening in camps had given him a knowledge of the heart's truth. The knowledge with which she was born, however, is of a different, a corrupted kind. It is a lost knowledge, but *because* of that she has power over him. Evidently "all things that touch the heart" which are "covered" by the heart's truth are not all things.

The ambiguous and abstract language by which the scene is rendered concentrates the reader's attention not upon the marriage act but upon the seduction, the offer of the "incredible promise" (312) of love and glory in exchange for the farm, upon Isaac's defeat before his lust, his inability to sustain his resolution, and then upon the final ironic twist of his wife's rejection not only of the land he had just paid as her price, but also of him, as she lies on her side, "her back to the empty rented room, laughing and laughing" (315).

The figure of Isaac's wife is vague. We are not told very much about her, only that she is "his wife," that she was "an only child, a small girl yet curiously bigger than she seemed at first, solider perhaps, with dark eyes and a passionate heart-shaped face" (311), and that she showed interest from the first in Isaac's farm. She is identified with the primeval and primigenial earth, yet her arm, like "a piece of wire cable" (314), holds him at bay until he promises to pay in civilization's coin. In this scene, though not earlier, she is thus something like Lion, identified with nature, yet impersonally engaged in a machine-like, single-minded pursuit of her goal which finally is to loosen the hold of the wilderness upon Isaac. The woman as corrupter for both Sam and Isaac has already been shown in earlier scenes. In "The Old People," Cass tells Isaac that Sam felt himself "betrayed" by the white blood in his mother, a quadroon slave, "not wilfully betrayed by his mother, but betrayed by her all the same, who had bequeathed him not only the blood of slaves but even a little of the very blood which had enslaved it" (168). The woman as corrupter is seen in Isaac's mother too. It was she who insisted that Uncle Buck move with her back into the big house when they were married, thus dislocating the Negroes whom Buck and Buddy had ceremoniously herded into the big house every evening in formal acknowledgement that the land was theirs, and it was Cass, descended from old Carothers through the female line, who tried to persuade Isaac to accept his tainted patrimony. Finally, and ironically, it is the wilderness as Isaac's "mistress and his wife" (326) which precludes his effective participation in civilized society.

Indeed, the narrator shows in Part V that his wife had a well-founded motive for jealous revenge upon the wilderness: "he would marry someday and they too would own for their brief while that brief unsubstanced glory which inherently of itself cannot last . . . but still the woods would be his mistress and his wife" (326). Prior to the bedroom scene, they *had* had their brief time of unsubstanced glory, a time, Isaac recalls in "The Fire and the Hearth," "when they voluntarily and in advance forgave one another for all that each knew the other could never be" (107-08). When he had married her, "it was the new country, his heritage too as it was the heritage of all, out of the earth, beyond the earth yet of the earth" (311), and their rented room was "wall-less and topless and floorless in glory" (311-12). But now, as she bargains, her whole body changes, becomes "composite of all woman-flesh" that ever "looked upon all the men who ever rutted" (314). With unpracticed movements "older than man" (314) she shows him that he cannot escape from the cable-strong pull of the earth's curse and proves him grandson of his grandfather.

V

Faulkner's narrative strategy in "The Bear" is, then, similar to that in *Absalom, Absalom!*. Through characters within the story and through the aesthetic organization, the initial romanticism is undermined and a final realism results. In *Absalom, Absalom!* Quentin's view of reality is both made credible and shown to be inadequate by placing it in the context of the author's larger and more inclusive reality, while in "The Bear" Isaac's romantic reading of his experience is rejected by the evaluations of Cass and the narrator. In some of its features the argument against Isaac is *ad hominem*. The fact that he cannot personally live the virtues of his wilderness vision is in itself no proof that they are not pertinent to the human situation. But insofar as he is shown to be inadequate to his vision by reason of his being human, then the case against him is *ad judicium*. Faulkner's criticisms of Isaac are as general as Isaac's claims. Isaac's failure is not peculiar to him; he is not a special case: we are all grandfather, all heirs of passion, and no man is ever free.

Faulkner does not wholly reject the theological content of Isaac's reading, but he does show its limitations. Isaac's understanding of the human condition is accepted, but not his "Christian" solution. Indeed, Faulkner shows his solu-

tion to be an illustration of the human situation rather than
an answer to it; his solution embodies a Christianity effectively undermined by Stoic assumptions about the nature
of man. Faulkner spins a very complex theological thread
in the story. "The heart's truth," in which Isaac feels he is
acting and from which the solution to the human condition
must come, would appear to be antithetical to Stoic rationalism; yet though Isaac sees no salvation in "what must
elect and choose," he inconsistently depends upon an act
of the will to effect salvation and thereby shows a disbelief
in the *radical* nature of that sin, or guilt, or curse, or old
world's taint by which he was able to account for the human
condition in the first place.

In other words, Isaac's diagnosis of the human condition
is Christian, but his solution to it is essentially Stoic, essentially one in which the reason and the will remain intact,
unaffected by the taint. Isaac assumes he can slough off the
sin and act in the heart's truth. That he is unable finally to
do so testifies to the accuracy of his diagnosis and to the fal-
lacy of his solution. At the same time it points up the tragic
inadequacy of even the heart's truth, for his heart gives him
the desire but not the capacity to fulfill it.

In setting up the romantic reading only to destroy it,
Faulkner moves toward a realism but does not in this story
offer a resolution of the human dilemma he has affirmed.
Much about the story is negative in implication. Nature is
no sure guide; one may respond to it in a variety of ways.
The human problem is moral but nature is amoral; it will
accommodate Boon as well as Sam, Lion as well as Ben;
Isaac's wife can be both the new country in glory and older
than man in rapacity. The heart's truth is not enough, though
it is a part of what will constitute a solution if there is one.
And a romantic retreat will not do. In an interview in Japan,
Faulkner voiced both the negative and the positive thematic

thrusts of "The Bear" when he rejected the idea that man could return to "an idyllic condition . . . free of trouble and sin." Mixing Stoic and Christian language, he said:

> I don't hold to the idea of a return. That once the advancement stops then it dies. It's got to go forward and we have got to take along with us all the rubbish of our mistakes and our errors [Stoic language]. We must cure them. . . . We must take the trouble and sin along with us [Christian language], and we must cure that trouble and sin as we go. We can't go back to a condition in which there were no wars, in which there was no bomb. We got to accept that bomb and do something about it, eliminate that bomb, eliminate the war, not retrograde to a condition before it exists, because then if time is a [forward] and continuous thing which is a part of motion, then we have to run into that bomb again sooner or later and go through it again. (*FN*, 77-78)

The positive implications of "The Bear" are sparse and they emerge only after a full recognition of the seriousness and extremity of the human condition. In a sense the South's (man's) sin and trouble, mistakes and errors, are a precious heritage. Faulkner feels toward the South's sin as Gavin Stevens feels toward the Snopeses: "it's for us to cope, to resist; us to endure, and (if we can) survive" (*T*, 102). Isaac's escape is neither possible nor desirable. Faulkner indicates no solution, no resolution, and certainly no rescue for man, but he does in this story indicate that one can live meaningfully by the courage of what might be called a Christian realism. Meaning comes by recognizing the guilt which makes the past a living present, accepting it as a burden, entering passionately into the stream of life, acknowledging the failure of justice to fulfill love, and grieving at the loss. Faulkner's strategy for meaning is dominantly that of a Christian humanist. Here, as elsewhere, he offers little beyond the meaning that morality with passion can bring.

V

Faulkner's Theology of Tension

I

As Faulkner criticism has matured, it has continued, among other things, to address itself in more detail to Faulkner's moral vision as it was initially isolated for study by O'Donnell, Cowley, and Warren. But it has also moved beyond that in the last dozen years to show a variety of intelligent critical responses to his religious core. It is no longer necessary to argue that Faulkner's works have a religious center; rather the task in this area of Faulkner analysis is to make a case for the kind of religiousness involved and to determine the degree of theological integrity in his fiction as a whole. The responses tend to fall into classic categories—skeptic, Stoic, humanist, Christian—and testify to the profusion of moral and religious insights to which Faulkner is capable of giving dramatic embodiment. The fact that the responses have been so diverse is solid witness to the complexity of Faulkner's theological core and a strong caution against too ready conclusions about the implications of his theological center for the Christian faith itself. My concluding remarks are made in the face of a formidable body of thought about Faulkner's achievement.

If the analyses offered in this study are cogent and just, they show at the least that from the beginning of his earliest mature work, Faulkner's rendered religious center is one of tension between Christian and Stoic visions. Yet, I believe that both our close and general looks at Faulkner would support the conclusion that his religious center is

169

essentially Christian humanism and that the humanistic side
of his Christian religiousness arises from his Stoicism. That
Faulkner is theologically cautious and conservative can be
seen in the constant qualification of his Christian and Stoic
visions by each other. The tension between them allows
the characteristic modern element of theological skepticism
also to find a place in his fiction. Faulkner seems unable to
tell the Christian story in isolation from Stoic insights, but
also unwilling to let his attachment to the tradition's Stoic
vision obscure the Christian judgment which explains its
failure to provide a lasting and meaningful moral order.
The Stoic tradition is judged from the point of view of a
Christian religiousness which admits its "truth" but does
not admit its unqualified adequacy and relevance.

In saying that Faulkner is a Christian humanist, that the
humanistic side of his Christianity arises from his sympathy
with the Stoic tradition, and that the tension between his
Stoicism and his Christianity allows the expression of a
theological skepticism, I do not intend to imply that he is
all things to all men. Rather, I intend to indicate the complexity of his theological center and to account for the variety
of critical responses to it. Albert Gérard, for example, sees
with good reason a new type of Stoicism in the endurance
with which Faulkner endows his heroes,[1] for it is a Christian
Stoicism—or better, a Stoic Christianity, since endurance and
pride and courage and compassion and sacrifice ultimately
have a Christian reference in Faulkner's fiction.

Hyatt Waggoner finds that the terms in which Faulkner
analyzes experience "are such as to make the historic Christian answers to the questions implicitly raised seem pertinent and natural."[2] But Waggoner could claim Faulkner is
Christian only in a limited sense, because although "in

---

[1] "Romanticism and Stoicism in the American Novel: from Melville to
Hemingway, and After," *Diogenes*, No. 23 (Fall 1958), 105.
[2] *William Faulkner: From Jefferson to the World*, p. 250.

Faulkner's works the crucifixion is central and paradigmatic,
. . . the resurrection might never have occurred. Grant all
objections that may reasonably be made at this point," Waggoner continues, "grant the difficulty of defining not only
'orthodoxy' but 'belief' of any sort, grant all this and more,
and it still remains true that the common core of belief that
has united Christians of all persuasions in all ages is ac-
ceptance of the miracle of the first Easter" (247).

In the best study of its type, Walter J. Slatoff continues
in a highly sophisticated manner the early response to
Faulkner as a theological skeptic, finding that Faulkner's
characteristic stylistic device of irresolution, the oxymoron,
extends to the structure and meaning of his novels.[3] Gérard,
Waggoner, and Slatoff (and other critics could serve equally
well as examples) point to something that is there in Faulkner—even Slatoff, who gives at once the most brilliant and
the least satisfactory total reading. The disorder, incoherence, irresolution, and ambiguity he isolates, and which
imply a skeptical view of life, function as foils for Faulkner's
more fundamental Stoic and Christian responses.

Although Faulkner does document a skeptical response
to modern experience, he does not rest there. His attachment
to the southern past combined with his understanding of its
failure in Christian terms leads him to move through skepticism to present the values he discerns in the tradition as
both possible and necessary for meaningful experience. Warren Beck puts the matter well when he says that Faulkner's
"genuine realism" "celebrates the saving mystery of man's
innate urge to postulate values and to react in terms of these
evaluations, in resistance to devaluation and in successive,
often ironic corrections of his own eccentricities."[4] The suc-

[3] *Quest for Failure: A Study of William Faulkner* (Ithaca: Cornell University Press, 1960); see especially the last chapter, "Conclusions."
[4] *Man in Motion: Faulkner's Trilogy* (Madison: The University of Wis-
consin Press, 1961), pp. 185-86.

cess of values postulated is not guaranteed in the nature of things. Men must, for Faulkner, achieve them themselves. And Faulkner's southern historical experience shows him that when they are achieved they are only tenuous, for they are constantly threatened by a strong tendency in men to corrupt, pervert, and fail in their finest vision. The tradition's failure results from men's tendency to make an idol of that very rationality which allows the vision, and thereby to lose the heart, the passion, the feeling, the human content which gives the vision its value.

Yet the fact remains that the values of the tradition are worth achieving. I believe that Faulkner does not equivocate on this point. His commitment to the meaning these values entail is the source of the brooding sense of loss, the wounding pain the author-reader-character feels when this meaning is absent. It is the source of the violence that erupts at the point where value is outraged. Even in the violence there is indication of an order, for the violence in his novels lays the nerve ends of life so bare that they are again sensitive to the meaning that is violated.

What all this adds up to is that Faulkner finds *in life* a recurrent flowing forth of meaningful possibility. Whitehead also saw such a phenomenon in experience and designated it as the function of God in his primordial nature. Faulkner is not that sophisticated theologically, but he has shown the same process artistically, and he has done so by bringing the full range of life's pathos into focus. One may say, using Tillich's theological image, that he documents that hell which is the strange way by which love works to open us up to the divine love. Faulkner, in other words, shows the processes of life seeking the conditions for salvation. If this much is true, then he shows morality approaching religion. As a Stoic, Faulkner believes the values in life are posited by men, but as a Christian he sees them attainable only in love.

The crucial question, then, is whether or not Faulkner sees life as redeemable if not redeemed, whether or not he has insight into the means by which the actual salvation is effected. Hyatt Waggoner implicitly poses the question of whether Faulkner gives us Easter as well as Good Friday. It is at this point that theological apologetics is most tempted to strain the evidence for a foregone conclusion that is either positive or negative. But what Faulkner has to say theologically is important only if he has really said it, has really rendered it dramatically. It is therefore here that criticism must be most cautious. There is no doubt but that Faulkner finds the Christian description of man as fallen to be in some sense a true one. There is no doubt but that man is a victim of himself as well as of circumstances. All three of our analyses support this much without ambiguity. Regarding the remainder of the question we have posed, I would suggest two things.

In the first place, Faulkner's contribution to the theological conversation may be made irrelevant if one poses the soteriological question in such a way that Faulkner is caught in an either/or trap, requiring either that he affirm a supernatural vision or that he end with a vastly attenuated Christianity. Such a formulation of the question is loaded, because the central debate on this question within the church itself, from Irenaeus and Augustine through Anselm, Abelard, and Luther to Rashdall and Aulén, has been over just what the work of Christ in fact was or is. The doctrine of the Atonement has remained a doctrine and has not become a dogma. And the correlative doctrine of the Incarnation (the Person of Christ as distinguished from his Work) has also been the subject of dispute. In other words, for those Christians outside of a received dogmatic tradition the content of Easter can be variously argued.

But this is, perhaps, to dodge an important question rather than to confront Faulkner with it, for it is a perfectly legitimate question to pose to one who seems to accept the first part of the Christian story as true. And if the question as formulated in the classical theological debate is asked of Faulkner, then I think that the response of his fiction is negative, yet negative with a protest, the protest recorded in *A Fable* where the runner (who is not named) muses:

> *In Christ is death at end in Adam that began:*—true, but the wrong one: not the wrong truth but the wrong moment for it, the wrong one needed and desired; clearing his mind again and making the attempt again, yet there it was again: *In Christ is death at end in Adam that*—still true, still wrong, still comfortless. (83)

Now, the runner's comfort is finally expressed in lines from Marlowe's *The Jew of Malta:* "but that was in another country;/and besides, the wench is dead." And such is Faulkner's conclusion too (though less cynically), but not his comfort. For Faulkner is radically disturbed that our received truths are not formulated with a coherence and relevance which make them speak powerfully for our "moment," our time. He embodies in his fiction the modern anguished disappointment, to which Camus and Hemingway also give powerful expression, that the traditional formulation of the resources for meaning gives us a hope contemporary experience too often fails to justify. He is able to entertain a vision of the human condition even more skeptical than the one implied by the runner's conclusion that that was in another time and place, and besides, God is dead. The extremity of man's condition in Faulkner—in a Quentin or a Hightower, a Christmas, a Jason, a Charlotte Rittenmeyer, a Horace Benbow, or the last Bayard Sartoris—is not simply that God is dead while man is still intact and able to function meaningfully; rather it is that in all meaningful ways man is dead too. God's death means the death of man. Such skepticism is ultimately rejected by Faulkner's Christian humanism, but it is in the face of such an expression of final meaninglessness that Faulkner finds it necessary to tell the Christian story, and it is because of the existential seriousness of such nihilistic skepticism that he finds the Christian story itself needs to be reformulated.

In the second place, then, Waggoner and others are right about Faulkner's discomfort in the face of an orthodox doctrine of the Resurrection. The positive form of his response to the doctrine is humanistic. He takes an option which the Easter-miracle-or-nothing form of the question does not allow, and that is to document in his fiction the tradition in Christianity which celebrates Easter as the good news of man's nature being fulfilled, being shown as existentially capable of what it essentially is. The doctrine of the Resurrection thus formulated is precious precisely because it does assume the human problem to be one of guilt rather than of foolishness, because it does speak to rather than deny man's actual nature. Faulkner responds in the same way as Charles Mallison to the Stoic proposition that "Man aint really evil, he jest aint got any sense." That leaves man, says Charles, "completely hopeless, completely worthless of anybody's anguish and effort and trouble" (M, 230). Rather, as the old Negro of A Fable puts it, "Evil is a part of man, evil and sin and cowardice, the same as repentance and being brave. You got to believe in all of them, or believe in none of them. Believe that man is capable of all of them, or he aint capable of none" (203).

"Flem Snopes," says Ratliff in The Mansion, "didn't deal in miracles: . . . he preferred spot cash" (141). Faulkner does not deal in miracles either, but prefers the reality he is able, as a modern and a Stoic man and a Christian, to perceive. Christian theology may, of course, find his perception simply myopic or distorted. But in any case, Faulkner's Stoicism leads him to emphasize that part of the Christian story which sees Christ as a normative example of what man can be in nature, life, and history by virtue of the for-

giving love of which he is capable. To put Faulkner's
Christian religiousness in this way is to strain his fiction by
theological language, but it is not, I believe, to be dishonest
about what, with all of Quentin's torments inside of him,
he has rendered through character in a Dilsey or a Lena
Grove or a Cass Edmonds or a Charles Mallison or the tall
convict and has achieved through the unity of symbol and
plot in the three stories we have studied closely.

II

It remains for us to look briefly at what Faulkner's
religious center implies for Christian theology. It is important, in such an inquiry, always to check what, humanly
or religiously speaking, we might want of Faulkner against
what we can get from him at the point of his greatest
strength. If I have assessed his religious center accurately,
then at least two possible implications of his aesthetic performance are important for the Christian faith.

Faulkner shows that it is possible for a great writer to
tell the Christian story, but only if it is done in responsible
relation to other aspects of our religious tradition and our
present situation. That is to say, as Preston Roberts of the
University of Chicago has so often put it, a great Christian
text is rarely simply Christian. Faulkner does not give up
his modernity and his Stoicism in order to make his stories
Christian, yet he does attempt to render the Christian story
with power. Faulkner deals with *the* questions: the source and
nature of evil, where and in what way and in the face of
what hazards there are resources for dealing with it. He
probes man's present dilemma by looking at its historical,
social, and psychological springs as well as by looking into
the private nature of man in a more directly theological
way. He is attentive to the violence and chaos apparent in

modern experience because it is in the face of that that man must live meaningfully if he is to live meaningfully at all. And probably most important for theology, he tries to test love under its most challenging conditions.

The fact that Faulkner does render the Christian story only in relation to other aspects of our experience means, in the second place, that a coherent and relevant retelling of the Christian story may require more careful attention to the inner complexity and richness of the Christian faith itself than contemporary theology is giving it. I do not mean to suggest that Faulkner himself has given as much care and attention as is necessary, for it may be that were he more profound theologically his rendered Christian vision would be able to break through the confines of its Stoic humanism. I am suggesting, however, that the failure of a great contemporary artist to tell the Christian story in its classic form and power points to unfinished business for Christian writers, critics, and teachers in our time. For Faulkner's inability to dramatize the Resurrection in its full power may be taken as a charge to the theological community, not simply to hold the Christian faith up before men, but to sustain and maintain a fuller balance within the Christian tradition itself, so that the Incarnation and the Resurrection may carry the same credibility for modern men as does the Fall. Not the least value of Faulkner is that he has not been able to render the Christian story whole, but has had to rearrange and qualify its content to give it aesthetic power.   . .

Index

179

McCaslin, Lucius Quintus Carothers, "old Carothers" (in *Go Down, Moses*), 140, 143, 146, 154, 155, 159, 160, 165

MacKenzie, Shreve (in *The Sound and the Fury*). See Shreve

Magny, Claude-Edmonde, 8-9, 12, 13, 22, 23

Mallison, Charles, Jr., "Chick" (in *The Mansion* and *The Town*), 21, 155-56, 161, 175, 176

Man, doctrine of: 3, 4; Faulkner's, 10, 18, 21-22, 82-83, 126, 127-28, 130, 166-68, 172-77; in Stoicism, 28-32, 82-83, 127-28, 130; in Christianity, 28-32, 130

The Mansion, 10, 12, 75, 78, 154, 155-56, 175

Marsh, John, 94-95

Melville, Herman, 147-48, 155

Method, literary: 4-6, 25; in *The Sound and the Fury*, 36-42, 68, 137; in *Absalom, Absalom!*, 101-07, 137; in "The Bear," 137-40, 166

Morality: and the southern tradition, 2, 55-56, 107-08; and religion, 3, 172

Moral vision, early use of the term, 2-3. See Faulkner, William

Mosquitoes, 35

Myth: Faulkner's use of, 8, 20-21; in "The Bear," 137, 139, 140, 141

Negro: in "The Bear," 12, 146, 148-49, 150, 156, 158-59; in *The Sound and the Fury*, 98-99; and Thomas Sutpen, 112, 122-25, 128-29; slavery, 128-31, 148

Neo-orthodoxy, 25

Niebuhr, Reinhold, 78-79, 131

Nobel Prize speech, 2

O'Connor, William Van, 156-57

O'Donnell, George Marion, 2, 7, 22, 169

O'Faolain, Sean, 7

"The Old People," 144, 151, 153, 165

Paine, Thomas, 18

Past: Faulkner's interest in, 2, 9, 45-46; for Quentin, 6, 9, 23, 61, 105-07, 121, 125; for lost characters, 9, 11, 23, 26; in *Absalom, Absalom!*, 105-06, 121. See Time; Tradition, southern

Perluck, Herbert A., 16, 158-59n, 160-62

Plato, 151, 152-53, 155

Process metaphysics, 5

Rashdall, Hastings, 173

Ratliff, V. K. (in *The Mansion*), 10, 175

The Reivers, 20, 35

Resurrection, 24, 26, 175, 177

Roberts, Preston T., Jr., 3, 176

Rosa (in *Absalom, Absalom!*), 5, 102-03, 109, 110, 118, 119, 130

Roth, Russell, 2, 3, 23

Russell, Bertrand, 29-30, 31

Salinger, J. D., 79

Salvation (soteriology): 9, 147, 156, 167, 172, 173; doctrine of, 3, 22, 32; in Christianity, 31-32, 126-28; in Stoicism, 31-32, 127-28

Sanctuary, 11, 35

Sartoris, 35, 44-45, 53

Sartoris, Bayard, "old Bayard" (in *The Unvanquished*), 45, 54-55, 56, 108-09, 111

Sartoris, Colonel John (in *The Unvanquished*), 45, 108-09, 111-12

Sartre, Jean-Paul, 9-12 *passim*, 22, 23

Scott, Nathan A., Jr., 3, 17